W9-BYZ-619

ADDITIONAL ADVANCE PRAISE FOR
THE TODDLER BRAIN

"This is such an important, timely, and assertive book. Presenting a wide range of relevant perspectives with professional insight and credibility, the fact that Dr. Jana's voice comes through as a warm and caring parent serves as the 'magic sprinkles' in this perfect recipe! This is a book that should be read by ALL parents and caregivers!"

> —Mine Conkbayir, Early Childhood researcher, lecturer, and author of *Early Childhood and Neuroscience*

"A compelling strategic plan for empowered parenting in the digital age, providing young children and parents with practical life enhancing tools for everyday brain building and 21st Century skill development."

> —Chip Donohue, PhD, Dean of Distance Learning & Continuing Education and Director of the TEC Center, Erikson Institute, and Editor, *Family Engagement in the Early Years*

"In this valuable work, Dr. Jana masterfully translates a wealth of compelling early brain and child development research to make this information accessible to parents and anyone else in the business of helping children succeed. This book is easy to understand and infinitely applicable so readers—and the children they care for—are likely to greatly benefit from it!"

> —Diana Fishbein, PhD, Co-Director, National Prevention Science Coalition to Improve Lives

"Powerful insights delivered in an engaging book that beautifully translates the latest research in early childhood into everyday parenting opportunities that will help children develop holistically and thrive in today's world."

> —Mark Greenberg, PhD, Bennett Chair on Prevention Science, Penn State University

"Highly compelling research into brain development and early childhood skills and abilities has now given us the best tools we have ever had for setting our children on successful life trajectories and ensuring they grow up to be smarter, healthier, and happier. This soon-to-be iconic book—written by a renowned pediatrician and parenting book author—helps point us in exactly that direction!"

> —George Halvorson, Chair-California's First Five Commission for Children and Families, Chair & CEO-Institute for InterGroup Understanding, Past Chair-Kaiser Permanente Health Systems

"More than anyone else I know, Dr. Laura Jana lives at the intersection of everything interesting. Is something happening in child development? Parenting? Business? Technology? Laura is there and listening and talking to people and learning and connecting one thing to another as only someone with her unique perspective can do. In *The Toddler Brain*, Dr. Jana brings you to where she lives: at the crossroads of everything amazing happening right now, from the explosion of brain science to the powers of mindfulness to the freshest ideas in business to the warmth of a mother's embrace. When all these ideas intersect the adventure of parenting becomes even more amazing and, fortunately, easier than you ever thought it could be."

> —David L. Hill, MD, FAAP, author of *Dad to Dad: Parenting Like a Pro* and Chair-AAP Council on Communications and Media

"Being a leader is like being a parent . . . being a parent is like being a leader. . . . Laura Jana's integration of workforce development terminology with child development will set the tone for ethical parenting (and leadership) practices for years to come!"

> —Beverly Kracher, PhD, Executive Director, Business Ethics Alliance, and Daugherty Chair in Business Ethics & Society, Creighton University

"This book will help you successfully unlock your child's cognitive and creative potential, not to mention your own powerful potential as a parent!"

> —Colleen Kraft, MD, pediatrician, Medical Director, Health Network at Cincinnati Children's

"As a school superintendent, I know the importance of children entering school ready to learn with engaged parents ready to support them. Dr. Jana has laid out a framework for parents and caregivers to prepare young children not only for success in school but also build a foundation for life."

> —Blane McCann, PhD, Superintendent, Westside Community Schools, Omaha, Nebraska

"At our organization, one of our core values is maximizing every child's potential. This book gives us the practical tools to do just that. I not only want to make this required reading for our staff, but would like to give every new family their own copy of the book. We are in this together to make a better future for all of our children."

> —Robert Patterson, CEO, Kids Can Community Center

"In *The Toddler Brain*, Dr. Laura Jana demonstrates and teaches 21st century skills by melding brain science, entrepreneurial innovation, and practical parenting to lay out a feasible and flexible strategic plan for raising the children of tomorrow to be their best, happiest, and most productive selves."

> —Michael Rich, MD, MPH "The Mediatrician," Director, Harvard Center on Media & Child Health

"By compellingly presenting the case for cultivating key life skills—or 'QI Skills'—early in life, Dr. Jana has captured the essence of the important shift in how we, as parents and collective communities, can best prepare our children for success and happiness in a rapidly evolving world."

> —Martin Scaglione, President & CEO, Hope Street Group; Former President & COO, ACT Workforce Division

"Reading *The Toddler Brain* will make both you AND your toddler smarter! In this innovative new parenting book, Dr. Laura Jana introduces the concept of "QI skills"—characteristics beyond just intelligence, or IQ, that can lead to future success as an adult. By starting to develop these important life skills early in infancy, you can give your child the best start possible. The essential parenting advice in *The Toddler Brain* will positively influence future generations for years to come. A must-read!"

> —Jennifer Shu, MD, pediatrician, CNNHealth, Medical Editor-American Academy of Pediatrics' HealthyChildren.org

"Very timely and useful! As a pediatrician and CEO who never stopped 'wiggling' and has a very long list of 'wobbles,' this book is the best I've seen on the why, how, and when of helping our children reach their full potential. Although great for toddlers, the insights and QI Skills defined in this book will undoubtedly benefit children (and adults) of all ages!"

> —Jeff Thompson, MD, pediatrician, CEO Emeritus-Gundersen Health System

"Dr. Laura Jana is a mover and shaker, a national treasure. Long may she write, speak, and inspire parents on the pathway to raising the best and brightest generation of children yet to come along."

> —Rosemary Wells, New York Times bestselling Children's Book author

"Describes in thoughtful parenting prose what we can do to best help young children develop the very same important human attributes now being clearly recognized as fundamental to adult success in the twenty first century."

> —Barry Zuckerman, MD, Chair Emeritus of Pediatrics, Boston University, Co-Founder of Reach Out & Read

THE
TODDLER
BRAIN

Also by Laura A. Jana

Heading Home with Your Newborn (with Jennifer Shu)

Food Fights (with Jennifer Shu)

Melvin the Magnificent Molar (with Julia Cook)

It's You and Me Against the Pee . . .
and the Poop Too! (with Julia Cook)

Amazing Me: It's Busy Being 3! (with Julia Cook)

The Surprising Science Behind Your Child's
Development from Birth to Age 5

THE
TODDLER
BRAIN

Nurture the Skills Today that Will Shape Your Child's Tomorrow

Laura A. Jana, MD

Da Capo
LIFE
LONG

Designed by Amy Quinn
Set in 12.25 point Joanna MT by Perseus Books

Cataloging-in-Publication data for this book is available from the Library of Congress.

First Da Capo Press edition 2017
ISBN: 978-0-7382-1875-5 (hardcover)
ISBN: 978-0-7382-1876-2 (e-book)

Published by Da Capo Press, an imprint of Perseus Books, LLC, a subsidiary of Hachette Book Group, Inc.

www.dacapopress.com

Da Capo Press books are available at special discounts for bulk purchases in the U.S. by corporations, institutions, and other organizations. For more information, please contact the Special Markets Department at Perseus Books, 2300 Chestnut Street, Suite 200, Philadelphia, PA 19103, or call (800) 810-4145, ext. 5000, or e-mail special.markets@perseusbooks.com.

10 9 8 7 6 5 4 3 2 1

This one's for you, Ajoy. You are my proof that it's not just children whose lives are forever changed by the gift of unwavering support and unconditional love!

CONTENTS

FOREWORD

by Jo Kirchner, CEO, Primrose Schools

YOU ARE HOLDING IN YOUR hands a book that could literally change the world. It's also a book I wish I could have written. Why? Because it so accurately reflects my strong belief that who children become is just as important as what they know. This belief serves as the guiding principle for the national family of over three hundred accredited early education and care schools across the country that I've had the privilege of leading for more than twenty-five years. As you'll learn on the following pages, research now confirms that this belief is more relevant than ever, as we prepare children for a complex world where empathy is just as important as literacy.

Laura Jana and I first met more than a decade ago when she became a Primrose School Franchise Owner. It did not take us long to discover that we shared a passion for quality early education infused with a balance of intellectual, social-emotional, physical, and life skills. Our friendship developed just as neuroscientists were uncovering the critical connection between early-life brain stimulation and a child's future success. As a pediatrician and renowned parenting expert, Laura's professional training and experience informed her perspective, while mine grew from a mother's intuition. Unlike Laura, however, I never planned on a career involving young children. It found me after a disappointing search for a high-quality preschool experience for my children. I didn't have a word for it back then, but I envisioned a place that would nurture not only academic skills, but also the qi, or positive life force, that Laura so powerfully defines in this book.

I love how *The Toddler Brain* weaves together the far-reaching but highly relevant principles of business, leadership, innovation, and the science of wellbeing with parenting. It will undoubtedly help parents and caregivers understand the critical role they play as the ongoing architects of their child's brain. A toddler's mental wiring develops faster in the first five years of life than it ever will again. These are crucial years to stimulate the neural connections that will embed not only a love of learning, but also the positive life skills required for success in the twenty-first century.

I am so proud of Laura for putting her wisdom into words that will benefit families everywhere. If readers follow her advice, today's children will be better equipped to solve tomorrow's challenges, and the world will be a kinder, more compassionate place.

PART 1

The Start-Up of Your Baby

> Our children are the rock on which our future will
> be built . . . The rich potential in each child must
> be developed into the skills and knowledge that
> our society needs to enable it to prosper.
>
> —Nelson Mandela, speech at the dedication
> of Qunu and Nkalane Schools, 1995

WHAT IF, DESPITE THE BEST of intentions, despite all our business-savvy, data-driven, technology-informed know-how and all that the Information Age has put right at our fingertips, we are, nevertheless, raising our children to succeed in a world that will not exist?

I am well aware this is not the typical way to start a parenting book. Especially not one meant to inspire parents of young children. Yet I have come to believe this single question raises what is perhaps the most critical issue that *all* twenty-first-century parents must consider. It is the question that should motivate us to think more strategically about the world our children will live in, better understand what skills they will need, and determine our role in more intentionally ensuring their success. It is also the question that compelled me to write this book.

Before taking on the task of addressing this question, however, allow me first to explain what, after more than twenty years in pediatrics and parenting, led me to ask it. After all, having been a practicing pediatrician and mother of three, the longstanding owner of a two-hundred-student educational child care center, a media spokesperson for the American Academy of Pediatrics, the founder of Practical Parenting Consulting, and the coauthor of two parenting books and three children's books (covering the topics of newborn care, nutrition, tooth brushing, potty training, and early childhood development), you could say that I was well situated and prominently involved in all aspects of practical, day-to-day parenting. That is, until a transformational conversation caused me to rethink my parenting worldview.

It was a couple of years ago, while attending a national conference, that I was introduced to a very highly accomplished fellow attendee who gave me a signed copy of his newly published book, and casually added, "I'd love to know what you think of it." I took his request seriously, read his book, and shared my thoughts. I told him that not only did his book read like an insightful parenting book but also it resonated particularly well with my own approach to the challenging task of raising productive children in the twenty-first century.

So far, this would seem like nothing terribly out of the ordinary, given that I have been both writing and reviewing parenting content for most of my professional career. What made this notably different, however, had to do with the part of the story that I left out: the fellow attendee was neither a pediatrician nor an established parenting expert. He wasn't even a parent. Rather, the book's author was none other than Silicon Valley visionary and LinkedIn cofounder Reid Hoffman. And it's safe to assume that his book, *The Start-Up of You*,[1] has never, and will never, pop up on any Amazon search for parenting books or show up on the shelves in the parenting section of any bookstore.

Now, if you're not familiar with *The Start-Up of You*, let me explain. Firmly established in the "Careers—Business &

Economics" category, the advice in this particular book is intended to strategically help readers "survive and thrive and achieve [their] boldest professional ambitions" by empowering them to become the CEOs of their own careers and control their own futures.

Despite what on the surface seemed like an admittedly vast divide between our professions and the shelves on which our books reside, the connection between Hoffman's convictions and my own regarding the critical need to identify the twenty-first-century toolkit of skills necessary to succeed was striking. So much so that it left me with the idea that perhaps what the parenting world could really benefit from is more of a "Start-Up of Your Baby" approach. While Hoffman and many others in the worlds of business, economics, leadership, and innovation are clearly identifying this modern-day toolkit of skills needed to succeed in today's emerging "creative economy,"[2] those of us in the business of raising children to be ready-for-life adults are ultimately responsible for and actively working to assemble this very same toolkit. We just work much farther upstream.

It is worth noting from the outset that although this book technically is titled *The Toddler Brain*, I propose that this upstream opportunity we have to start assembling our children's contemporary toolkit actually begins surprisingly early, even before they begin to stand on their own two feet. Sure, toddlerhood tends to be when the fruits of our early labors become more outwardly apparent as our protégés begin to more actively toddle, talk, and reach out to touch the world around them. But the fact of the matter is that successful brain building and mental mastery can and should start long before toddlerhood (and, for that matter, extend well past it!). Every parent needs to be aware of three key takeaways from the latest science in brain and child development:

1. The opportunity for foundational brain building begins right from day one.

2. The entire period leading up to toddlerhood and extending several years past it—specifically, between birth and age five years—offers us an unparalleled window of opportunity to facilitate the assembly of an invaluable set of life-enhancing twenty-first-century skills that will serve our children well throughout their entire lives.

3. Yes, the first five years are critically important, but brain building and skill building by no means end at age five. Rather, your efforts represent the start of a lifelong parenting commitment that can be kept all the more successfully when it rests on a strong, early foundation!

In an age when everyone is clamoring for innovative ideas, it has been said that the best chance for groundbreaking innovation occurs when diverse concepts, disciplines, and industries collide.[3,4] I suggest that the parenting world is on the verge of just such a groundbreaking "collision," where business, economics, and workforce development are colliding with neuroscience, child development, psychology, and pediatrics to generate a powerful new set of shared twenty-first-century skills critical for success in today's complex, rapidly changing, globalized, technology- and data-driven world. As everyone from CEOs to economists and educators sets their sights on these critical skills, innovative parents will recognize the incredible opportunities now before us: the opportunity for brain building; the opportunity for cultivating these skills early; and the opportunity for applying what we now know about today's world to more purposefully parent our children for success starting from the day we head home with our newborns.

The Power of Mental Mastery

According to eminent developmental psychologist Lev Vygotsky, children's mastery of mental tools early in life has the power not only to transform their cognitive skills and enable them to take charge of their own learning in an intentional and purposeful way but also to transform their physical, social, and emotional skills such that they can become masters of their own behavior as well.

A Strategic Parenting Plan

FOR DECADES, IF NOT CENTURIES, parents have bemoaned the fact that babies don't come with an owner's manual—a wish that by its very nature implies it is possible to precisely predict, plan, and prepare for every potential parenting challenge that might come our way as we strive to raise our children to live, learn, and thrive in a networked world. Yet the fact of the matter is that this is no longer possible, much less realistic. As Hoffman notes in his book, "You are changing, the people around you are changing, and the broader world is changing—so it's inevitable the playbook will evolve and adapt."[5]

Rather than an owner's manual that addresses the *how* and the *what* of parenting, I therefore suggest that what today's parents really need is a playbook in the form of a strategic plan, one that continually reminds us of *why* it is we do what we do, clarifies what it is we are ultimately aiming to accomplish, offers actionable goals to help guide us, and at the same time allows us to be flexibly persistent when faced with new parenting challenges.

As author Jennifer Senior reinforces in her book *All Joy and No Fun*, "Parenting may have become its own activity (its own profession, so to speak), but its goals are far from clear."[6] With a thousand issues clamoring for precious hours in the day, committing time as parents to planning for the future is admittedly difficult. But operating without a plan is even more challenging. This last thought, by the way, comes almost word-for-word from yet another highly unlikely, yet surprisingly relevant book: *Business Plans For Dummies*.[7]

Recognizing that our changing world demands a parenting shift from owner's manual to strategic plan is a big step in the right direction. But taking it a step further, what if we were to develop a real, usable strategic parenting plan—one that infuses us with a sense of purposeful action and provides a North Star for us to follow as we approach the day-to-day decisions and challenges of parenthood? Doing so would simply involve a review of the core elements of a strategic plan and their application not to a company but to the business of parenting.

Before getting started, however, it's worth noting the difference between strategic versus long-range planning. According to the strategic-plan-focused *For Dummies* book, long-range planning (much like an owner's manual) is based on the assumption that current knowledge about future conditions is sufficiently reliable.[8] As we will discuss in Chapter 2, this is a false assumption that no longer serves us well in business or in parenting. In contrast, strategic plans, which by definition are designed explicitly to be responsive to a dynamic, ever-changing environment, are much better suited for today's world and for our parenting needs.

Every strategic plan consists of the same basic elements:

- A mission and vision statement
- A description of long-term goals

- Strategies for achieving these goals
- Action plans for implementation

In a parenting context, that is exactly what the book you're now holding offers.

Let's start with mission and vision. When it comes to crafting a single sentence that clearly captures the inspirational long-term results we hope to achieve as a result of our parenting efforts, raising our children to be happy, healthy, successful adults represents as universal a vision statement as any. But true to strategic planning form, we shouldn't stop there.

In setting our sights on more specific big-picture parenting goals, research from Gallup can help us more clearly identify five essential elements of the overarching concept of well-being: career, financial, social, physical, and community.[9] All five are important and clearly interconnected. But, for the purposes of this strategic parenting plan, let's start by taking a closer look at career success, a focus that you will soon discover inevitably leads us straight to the twenty-first-century skills and brain-building strategies required to achieve it.

To help bring all the elements of our strategic parenting plan together in an easy-to-follow framework, it makes good sense to address the following three basic yet clarifying questions: *Where are we now? Where are we going?* and, last but perhaps most important, *How will we get there?*[10]

WHY US This chapter serves the purpose of asking *Where are we now?* It offers an important assessment of the current state of parenting affairs that includes a discussion of how to build on our strengths and capitalize on opportunities while also giving necessary consideration to potential parenting weaknesses and threats to our ultimate goal of raising children to become ready-for-life adults.

WHY NOW Answering this question involves taking a much broader look at the increasing complexity of our rapidly changing world than what is typically found on the pages of parenting magazines, books, and blogs. By looking up from our day-to-day parenting realities and assessing what has changed from when we were young and from the last century to this one, we end up with a much clearer and more relevant picture of the world our children will be living in.

WHY EARLY Armed with important insights and a list of highly valued skills from WHY NOW, WHY EARLY helps formulate an innovative parenting strategy by addressing the critical question *How will we get there?* This includes, first and foremost, a description meant to reassure you that this book is in no way yet another tiger mom or helicopter parenting book. After making perfectly clear what starting early is *not* about, WHY EARLY offers an overview of the compelling early childhood and baby brain science behind twenty-first-century skill building that promises to pull together in even greater and more intriguing detail all of the surprising science behind your child's earliest development. WHY EARLY also offers clear objectives and actions that all parents can use to build these skills and reinforces the incredible opportunity we have to equip our children, starting in the earliest years of their lives, with the twenty-first-century toolkit of skills we now know all children will need to succeed.

WHY US

The Current State of Parenting Affairs

If your actions create a legacy that inspires others
to dream more, learn more, do more and become
more, you are an excellent leader.

—Dolly Parton

Be my teacher from day one
Be my sky, my moon, my sun.

—Rosemary Wells, *Hand in Hand*

I N 1946, DR. BENJAMIN SPOCK published the first edition of
his book *Baby and Child Care*.[1] At the time, it was virtually the
only book of its kind on the market, and it continued to be so
for several decades to follow. The parenting world was hungry
for his tome, and Dr. Spock soon came to be recognized as the
most trusted pediatrician of his time. His influence was so far-
reaching that for much of the last century many parents considered his book to be the parenting "bible." And after its more than
five decades in print, *Baby and Child Care* was in fact recognized as

one of the best-selling books in the history of the world, second only to the Holy Bible.[2]

I was fortunate enough to have witnessed firsthand the effort Dr. Spock put forth in providing parents with all of the basic how-to's of baby care and teaching the fundamentals of child development. I had the privilege of working with him in the 1990s, first as a medical student and later as a consultant as he completed what would turn out to be the last revisions he made to his book before he passed away on March 15, 1998. In looking past just his parenting book, however, it is clear that Dr. Spock offered parents something that extended well beyond his practical, detailed, carefully explained advice. In convincing parents to "Trust yourself. You know more than you think you do," his words were embraced by new parents around the world, empowering them throughout his lifetime and for generations to come.

Trusting Yourself

EMPOWERING PARENTS IS AS RELEVANT and fundamentally valuable a goal today as it was throughout Dr. Spock's reign as "The World's Pediatrician,"[3] if not more so. That said, the world has changed significantly since his time, and being able to sincerely and reassuringly convince parents today that we actually do know more than we think we do is a very different proposition. With 24/7 news cycles, a constant barrage of bits of parenting advice randomly splayed across books, blogs, magazines, message boards, websites, Twitter feeds, Facebook posts, and more, obtaining parenting information today can seem a lot like trying to drink water from a fire hose. Rather than quenching your thirst, it's easy to feel like you're drowning. In short, the problem is we're living in an age of information overload.

This creates an echo-chamber-like effect in which ideas and information—parenting advice included—are continuously repackaged and recirculated long after they've reached their expiration date of being relevant, if they ever were. Although we may have the world at our fingertips and greater access to more information than ever before, what poses a real threat to modern-day parenting success and our ability to trust ourselves is, in part, the widespread lack of distinction between information and knowledge.

Not all information is created equal, and with so much parenting information swirling around us, it's often difficult (if not impossible) to tell what's reliable and fact-checked. Parents run the risk of trying to take it all in without being able to adequately filter out the contaminated, dangerously inaccurate, or fear-inducing hyperbole. As behavioral neuroscientist and author of The Organized Mind[4] Daniel Levitin puts it, "We are overloaded with junk . . . [and] it's becoming harder and harder to separate the wheat from the digital chaff."[5] Parents today are left feeling like they know less than ever. Confused and overwhelmed, parents have become conditioned to constantly question, compare, and even compete among ourselves as we search for answers, reassurance, and validation. And with helicopter parents and tiger moms in the mix, the competition can seem mighty tough.

In the half century after Dr. Spock wrote the first edition of Baby and Child Care, parents used to confidently say, "Dr. Spock helped me raise my child." Now there are literally thousands of titles in the parenting space, and although they continue to multiply at an impressive rate, they're failing to instill that same sense of confidence. Today I hear parents lament that they've read "all" the baby books out there and still feel lost at every turn. The onslaught of information is making us feel less empowered than ever. To be able to truly trust ourselves, we need to think clearly and strategically about what we're doing and why we're doing it, and then establish a clear plan of action for ourselves. Beyond the day-to-day aspects of parenting, this plan will guide us toward finding the answers we need and instill in us the ability to adapt when inevitable parenting challenges arise.

Switching Gears:
From Owner's Manual to Strategic Plan

WHILE CRADLING A FRESHLY SWADDLED newborn, it is a rare parent who doesn't wish babies came with an owner's manual. After all, there's nothing quite like the reality and unfamiliarity of heading home with a newborn to immerse new parents in the here-and-now of parenthood. In an effort to introduce parents to this "brave new world" and help guide them through it, I coauthored a book akin to an owner's manual, *Heading Home with Your Newborn*.[6] My aim was—and continues to be, as the book heads into its third edition more than ten years later—to provide parents with a trusted source of critically important, much-needed, and commonly sought-after information, especially during those early days. Even while writing it, however, my goal wasn't to give parents everything they'd ever need to know or answer every possible question that might arise about how their babies "work." In fact, I didn't want parents to feel like they needed to carry my book (or anyone else's) in their back pocket at all times. Rather, my goal has always been to provide parents with enough information to build a foundational framework they can use to make their own best decisions about caring for and raising their children.

Once you're up to speed on the nuts and bolts of parenting, the next necessary step in making parenting decisions is making sure you also take time to remember your bigger picture and purpose: how to help your child develop into a ready-for-life adult. Although it's understandably tempting to put off thinking about this all-encompassing goal until a later date—preferably one that no longer involves diapers, crying, and spoon-feeding—waiting until after you've made your way through the early (and admittedly most overwhelming, tiring, and physically taxing) years puts you at risk for potentially missing out on having a tremendously positive early impact on your child's future.

To maximize these crucial early years, I propose a much more empowering approach. That approach begins with a review of the current state of parenting affairs. In doing so, we'll take a motivational look at our parenting strengths and opportunities as well as an honest look at our potential parenting weaknesses and threats to our parenting success and how best to avoid or overcome them.

The Most Important Job(s) in the World

ONE OF THE GREATEST OPPORTUNITIES we have going for us as parents is that we hold not one but *several* of the most important jobs in the world. We serve as highly influential role models. We are our children's first and, if we do our job well, very best teacher. And if we rise to the challenge of engaging our children day in and day out—an approach we'll discuss further in WHY EARLY that has a far greater impact than simply keeping them entertained or out of trouble—we also earn ourselves the long-overdue distinction of CEO: Chief Engagement Officer. These positions share the same job description of raising ready-for-life adults, and each offers us the opportunity to assume a whole host of pivotal roles in our children's lives. Wrap all these roles together and it's not surprising that parents today are being recognized as ultimate leaders.

Although Simon Sinek's book *Leaders Eat Last* isn't about parenting per se, the title alone conjures up an image of what it means to be a parent—after all, what hungry parent hasn't pulled together a meal of scraps long after their child has been fed, bathed, read to, cuddled, and put to bed?[7] Sinek shares my underlying belief that everything about being a leader is like being a parent, recognizing that we are the ones, after all, who fully commit to the well-being of those in our care. We're willing to run headfirst into the unknown, rush toward danger, and routinely put our children's best interests before our own in what can be viewed as a real-world game of follow-the-leader, a game we can "win" if we stay true to our course.

You've Got Their Whole World in Your Hands

FROM THE DAY WE ENTERTAIN the idea of taking on the world's most important job as parents, one of our greatest strengths becomes our unconditional love for and unwavering commitment to our children. We want to give them the world and are willing to do just about anything to achieve this noble goal. It is this dedication, after all, that sends us on our parental quest for answers, keeps us up at night, and has us calculating the cost of college tuition right around the same time we start comparing the cost of cribs. It's what causes us to turn our lives upside down and redefine our purpose.

Yet in today's world of guilt-driven, competitive parenting, what has long represented our greatest strength now runs the very real risk of becoming a threat unless we carefully consider what *best* really means. We need to realize that wanting what's best for our children doesn't mean giving, doing, or answering everything for them. Nor is it synonymous with coddling them or keeping them happy at all costs. All too often *best* also gets translated into clearing all obstacles from our children's path without realizing that their ability to overcome obstacles is integral to their growth and development. To capitalize on our greatest strength—our unconditional love for and commitment to our children—we need to keep in mind that parenting is a delicate balancing act. Giving our children the best is about maximizing their potential, not their possessions; it's about cultivating their sense of purpose and passion, not subjecting them to unnecessary pressure; and it's about fulfilling our role as protectors without becoming so overprotective that our kids are never allowed to trip, stumble, or tumble and, as a result, miss out on experiencing what it takes to get back up again.

Giving Parenting a Real-World Checkup

ALTHOUGH I WHOLE-HEARTEDLY BELIEVE IN the power of positive parenting, it's important to take a realistic assessment of several common ailments that routinely plague today's parenting world. These parenting "diagnoses" can be contagious and, when allowed to spread unchecked, can really knock parents off course and take a toll on the very well-being of our best-laid plans. Fortunately, simply being aware of the risks works wonders for taking the necessary steps to effectively immunize ourselves against them. These parenting-world afflictions can be broken down into the following four primary conditions:

- **Breath holding.** This ailment is characterized by the tendency, upon entering new parenthood, to put our heads down, hold our breath, and hope for the best as we simply aim to survive the next five (or eighteen) years. A single-frame cartoon I came across several years ago all-too-accurately illustrates what this particularly common ailment can look like: a harried-looking mom in a cluttered kitchen, accessorized by a toddler hanging on her shirt and an infant wailing on her hip, stands with a phone to her ear and a caption that reads, *Can I call you back in five years?*[8]

- **Nearsightedness.** An equally common condition in which the further into the future our parenting goals extend, the more likely they are to become blurry and hard to keep in sight. Although parenting nearsightedness can become chronic if parents don't learn to broaden their focus, this short-term thinking is most common in the earliest years of raising children when all of the crying, clothing, car seats, and diapers understandably cause us to lose sight of our parenting big picture. This singular focus on the here-and-now without any added big-picture perspective qualifies as a "Parent's Dilemma"[9] because it causes parents to get lost in the short term and (at the risk of mixing potentially unfamiliar metaphors) stuck in the parenting equivalent of living by quarterly earnings.

- **Chronic parenting fatigue (CPF).** At the outset, a certain degree of parental sleep deprivation is inevitable. But what makes this condition dire is the persistent feeling of being overwhelmed, frustrated, worn out, and chronically stressed long after your baby starts sleeping through the night. Contributing causes to the development of CPF include helicopter or tiger parenting, the so-called mommy wars, and participation in the perceived race through childhood that involves pushing our children to achieve milestones earlier, faster, better and to get everything right the first time. In addition to leaving parents feeling stricken with the accompanying symptoms of parental self-doubt or guilt, attempting to keep pace with all of this constant competition and comparison is, quite frankly, just plain *exhausting*. When allowed to take hold, CPF and all that it entails can threaten our confidence as well as our ability to stay committed to our ultimate purpose.

- **Social deficit disorder (SDD).** Today, parents are more likely than generations past to find ourselves far away from our families or any sort of "village" to help us raise our children. As a result, this contemporary disorder is characterized by feelings of isolation and separation from the social connections and support that we know to be so vital for our overall well-being. It also involves accepting the false perception of parenthood as an inherently necessary departure from the real world. The risk associated with failing to interact with the world outside of just work and all of the many play dates, preschool activities, and other experiences directly related to the parenting sphere is that parents' worldview becomes increasingly narrow. If left untreated, parents eventually lose touch with the very world in which they're raising their children to inhabit.

To remedy these modern-day parenting woes that all too often come to define new parenthood, we need to stay true to our bigger parenting purpose. By definition, parenting with purpose means beginning with the end in mind, a strategy that, according to Stephen Covey, author of The 7 Habits of Highly Effective People, means we need to begin each day, task, or project with a clear vision of our intended direction and destination, and then continue flexing our proactive parenting muscles to make things happen.[10] This is what having a strategic parenting plan is all about.

So, Why Us?

THE POWERFUL COMBINATION OF YOUR unwavering parental commitment to your child's well-being along with the many early and influential roles that you will juggle (not only in the same day but often at the same time) on your child's behalf puts you at the exact right time and right place for what is proving itself to be an unrivaled opportunity. As you'll see in more detail in WHY EARLY, scientists are finding that in your role as parent—well beyond protector and provider of your child's basic survival necessities (food, water, shelter, and safety)—you actually stand to cultivate key skills and shape your baby's brain in ways that will set your child up for future success. So, when it comes to answering the question, *Why us?* well, it is us—as our children's parents, protectors, providers, role models, teachers, leaders, and CEOs—who are perfectly situated to have the most profound and lasting impact on our children's lives starting from the day they're born.

If we're in agreement that our ultimate goal is to raise our children to live, learn, and thrive in today's world, then our natural next step involves looking up from our parenting trenches to find out what's going on in the greater world around us and identifying the toolkit of skills our children will need to succeed. That leads us to WHY NOW.

WHY NOW

The World Our Children Will Live In

A billion hours ago, modern Homo sapiens emerged . . .

A billion seconds ago, the IBM personal computer was released.

A billion Google searches ago . . . was this morning.

—Hal Varian, Google's chief economist, National Association for Business Economics (NABE) Annual Meeting, September 10, 2013

COMMITTING TO MORE STRATEGICALLY HELPING our children reach for the stars means that we need to shift our attention, however briefly, away from the here-and-now of parenthood and gain clarity about the world in which our children will be living.

The first time I read *The Start-Up of You*, it solidified what I'd become increasingly aware of in recent years: that the parenting and business spheres weren't so far apart. Intrigued, I dedicated myself to learning more about what was happening in the fields of business and innovation. I absorbed what others were concluding in sources such as the *Harvard Business Review, Fortune,* and *Inc.* as well as researched industry leaders from Google to Gallup. The more I compared these worlds to the parenting world I knew so well, the stronger the connections became between the skills today's businesses were after and the skills those of us in the parenting world were working hard to cultivate in our children. In fact, with titles like "Don't Pamper—Engage!"[1] *Building Resilience,*[2] and *Playing to Win,*[3] it became increasingly difficult to distinguish which "world" the latest literature was even coming from. Today, the synergies are stunning. Whether you open a business journal, the *New York Times,* or the business section of a local newspaper, the direct relevance between business and parenting, and between workforce development and early learning, is popping up everywhere.

As we work to figure out where we are going and how best to achieve our parenting goals, now is the time to take a moment to look beyond the traditional parenting space, with all of its books, blogs, and baby-and-me classes; make note of the significant changes in the greater world around us; and adapt how we approach parenting accordingly. And that's exactly what we're about to do.

What Just Happened?

A GOOD WAY TO ESTABLISH the need for a shift in how we parent our children is to simply take a look around us and ask, *What just happened?* In the simplest terms, the Information Age is what happened. Left behind is an Industrial Age characterized by assembly-line, one-size-fits-all, linear ways of approaching the world. We've now raced headfirst into an age that, true to its name, has a whole lot to do with incredible amounts of information and unrivaled access to it. As parents navigating an environment overrun with endless amounts of parenting information on every topic Google-able, we're well aware of and experiencing firsthand the dizzying effects of this information revolution on a daily basis.

However, putting information at our fingertips represents only part of the story of what just happened. The Information Age is also recognized as the Digital Age for good reason. Since the 1990s, the rapid rise of computers and what has been referred to as "the relentless march of technology"[4] is credited with unmistakably defining and driving this rapidly evolving period in human history. Advances in technology are also enabling us to tackle challenges, innovate, and create new, customized solutions faster, easier, cheaper, and smaller than ever before. As for the impact this will have on how we parent our children, Harvard media researcher and pediatric colleague Michael Rich puts it best when he describes technology as now being like the air our children breathe. Yes, it runs the risk of contamination, but it's here to stay and our children's success will depend on not only learning to use it wisely but also developing those skills most valued in a technology-driven world.[5]

When we consider our purpose as parents to prepare our children to succeed within this "brave new world," the path becomes both clear and admittedly a bit daunting: we need to look beyond IQ and focus on cultivating a new set of skills that includes being able to seamlessly adapt to change.

Beyond IQ

AS THE TWENTIETH CENTURY TRANSITIONED from farms to factories, businesses, and offices, the role of the "knowledge worker" emerged. Intellect became a highly prized quality within the workplace, and, in turn, IQ became a tool for measuring it. Nowadays, however, we're finding that being "book smart," although still important, isn't sufficient on its own. Nor, for that matter, is IQ deemed useful as a sole metric for effectively predicting future success. As noted in *Harvard Business Review,* "In the era of Wikipedia, does it really matter how much you can memorize? What's more important is that you can take the perspective of others. In this way, empathy is the new literacy: essential for us to communicate, collaborate, and lead."[6]

In addition, the complex and global nature of the challenges we face today are considered too complicated for any one person to solve on his or her own. This has resulted in an even greater value placed on the ability to connect, coordinate, and work well with others across professions, cultures, and continents. It's important to note that the emphasis placed on these social and relationship skills is not to the exclusion of IQ. Rather, these non-cognitive skills, also referred to as *soft* skills, are now deemed necessary in *addition* to those that make up our more traditional definitions of intellect.

As counterintuitive as it might seem, technology has also had a hand in the rise of empathy in the workplace. Although there are some pretty "smart" technologies available to help us with facts, figures, calculations, and cognition, we are still, for the most part, left to our own devices when it comes to aspects of the human touch that define these more social and emotional skills. In fact, it is predominantly the jobs that require both cognitive *and* soft skills that are experiencing the most growth today. And as more and more jobs become automated and as machines are able to do many tasks cheaper, faster, and better than humans can, it is predicted that those occupations that require these "other" skills—as well as the people who possess them—are the ones that won't be replaced any time in the foreseeable future.[7]

Planning to Adapt

IN THE PREVIOUS CENTURY, CHANGE also happened in a mostly linear, predictable fashion in which each new development seemed to build upon its predecessor. Having a ten-year plan to plot one's professional course was expected: like on an escalator, people moved steadily up within their careers, so they could realistically set their sights on where they wanted to be within the next decade.[8] Today, however, change is happening at such a mind-boggling pace that knowing exactly what we're aiming for is like trying to hit a moving target—whether that target represents our professional or our parenting goals. To put this accelerating rate of change into perspective, it's been estimated that 65 percent of children today will end up in jobs that have yet to be invented.[9] Although we may not know the specific jobs, industries, or trades they will occupy, much less the tools they will use to perform them, what we can predict is the need for agility and other abilities such as curiosity, creativity, critical thinking, and executive function skills that will enable our children to seamlessly adapt.

Being adaptable also means being able to put large amounts of information into context in order to make sense of it. The necessity of this skill represents another sizable shift from the last century, where we became exceptionally adept at distilling, concentrating, isolating, and siloing everything from our professions to our pills down to their smallest, most granular forms. In the Information Age, however, it's no longer about just defining the details but about knowing how to integrate them in order to make sense of them. Whereas last century saw us setting our sights on sequencing the entire human genome base pair by base pair, for example, today putting genes back into the context of their environments has given rise to the new and profoundly important field of epigenetics. Seeing the bigger picture is also proving key for innovating new products, new ideas, and new solutions—some of the defining features of the current century.

In other words, as Pulitzer Prize–winning author and journalist Thomas Friedman so clearly sums up, "Something really big happened in the world's wiring in the last decade . . . [as] the combination of . . . connectivity and creativity has created a global education, commercial, communication and innovation platform on which more people can start stuff, collaborate on stuff, learn stuff, [and] make stuff . . . with more other people than ever before."[10]

The New Guiding Principles

AS LEADERS AND CHIEF ENGAGEMENT Officers dedicated to better connecting what we do today with what we want for our children's tomorrow, we need to shift our parenting perspective to be in alignment with the ever-changing, rewired world around us. Based on the profoundly simple observation made by Lev Vygotsky, the Soviet psychologist who founded the theory of biosocial development, that how we educate our children must be oriented not toward the yesterday of a child's development but toward its tomorrow, the following are ten guiding principles borrowed straight from the twenty-first-century world of business and innovation that will enable us to better chart our parenting course.

1. **Put people and purpose first.** Businesses are recognizing the need to shift their focus from the *how* and the *what* to a more purpose-driven *why* approach or face falling behind.[11, 12] This reprioritization is reinforced by a Global Deloitte survey that found Millennials to be just as interested in how businesses

develop their people and contribute to society as they are in their products and profits.[13]

2. **Engage, don't pamper.** When it comes to both employee well-being and the business bottom line, workplace pampering and indulgences are no substitute for engaging workers. According to Gallup's chief scientist of workplace management and well-being, the feeling of being a part of something significant that engagement brings has positive performance consequences for teams and organizations.[14]

3. **Consider collaboration as the new competition.**[15] In a world of increasing complexity and interconnectedness, leaders, organizations, and businesses alike are recognizing that individual best efforts can't compete with the power of collaboration and collective impact in a sharing economy.

4. **Recognize the value of play at work.** Although it has long been recognized that play is the "work" of three year-olds, in days past we have seen play as something we need to grow out of as we learn to take our work "more seriously." Nowadays, however, work is becoming a lot more like preschool[16] as we discover that applying social skills, games, and open-ended play to our daily work is good for everything from creative thought and employee morale to workplace productivity.

5. **Embrace nonlinear thinking.** With big value placed on creative and innovative ideas, linear thinking and following a straight and narrow path have gone by the wayside as interest shifts to the ability to color outside the lines and think in nonlinear (divergent) ways.

6. **Rely on compasses instead of maps.**[17] In a world defined by unpredictability and change, it is far more valuable to be able to adapt and chart your own course than it is to be reliant on a static road map.

7. **Prioritize questions over answers.** With the entirety of the world's information virtually at our fingertips, simply knowing

the right answer is no longer what counts. It's being able to ask the right questions that does.

8. **Gain big-picture perspective.** Focus is what helped us generate all of our discoveries, data, and details about the world. The name of the game today is the ability to put all of these pieces back together and back into their bigger-picture context.

9. **Learn to read people.** We have now entered the "golden age of empathy"—a world in which emotional intelligence, relationships, and the ability to read other people (collectively known as "EQ") that have surpassed stand-alone IQ and traditional book smarts.

10. **Be willing to get it wrong.** One of innovation's most important truisms is that you can't innovate if you're not prepared to fail. With this awareness comes a significant shift away from simply playing it safe and getting it right toward intelligent risk taking and learning to fail forward.[18]

WHY EARLY

Baby Brain Science and the Foundational Importance of Starting Early

It is in the first 1,000 days of life that the stage is set for fulfilling individual potential.

—Roger Thurow, *The First 1,000 Days: A Crucial Time for Mothers and Children— and the World*

If we change the beginning of the story, we change the entire story.

—Dimitri Christakis, "Media and Children," TEDxRainier, 2011

IN MARCH 2001, CONGRESS CONVENED to address the country's economic circumstances. A somewhat unusual discussion ensued after a seasoned politician took the floor and began his comments with the opening statement, "Mr. President, I came across one of my favorite books last evening . . . most people in this country have read this book or seen the book . . . [and]

I started thinking about [it] in the context of the grappling that we do in this country with our economy."[1] His assumption that most people had seen or read the book to which he was referring was hardly an exaggeration. It had, in fact, rocketed up the *New York Times* Best Sellers list. What was a bit unusual in this context, however, was the fact that the book was *All I Really Need to Know I Learned in Kindergarten*.

In it, author Robert Fulghum offers a list of lessons typically taught in American kindergartens, suggesting that the world would be a much better place if only adults adhered to the same basic rules as five-year-olds.[2] Included on this list, along with some more practical reminders like taking a nap every afternoon and always remembering to flush, are more pertinent skills such as sharing, playing fair, keeping your hands to yourself, and remembering to take in the world around you with an appreciative sense of wonder. Reinforcing Fulghum's sentiment, the senator wove specific lessons from the book all throughout his talk, pointing out to his congressional colleagues, "We forget the most basic of things—almost kindergarten-like lessons . . . so very quickly." As the senator finished addressing what he described as the largest economic deficit in American history, he concluded, "It is not rocket science to fix this. Again, all we really need to know we learned in kindergarten."

The essence of these insights still applies today, but with two very important contemporary updates. The first is that, although making the connection between twenty-first-century skills and early childhood foundations may not be rocket science, it most certainly is brain science. The other involves recognizing that in looking at kindergarten as our starting point for encouraging the development of these skills, we simply haven't been looking early enough. A foundationally significant amount of what our children need to know they actually start learning well *before* kindergarten, during the first five years of their lives.

What is now understood about our children's earliest abilities is worthy of both our parental attention and our amazement. Born as truly global citizens with the potential to communicate in any language; the ability to read and interpret emotions during their earliest days, weeks, and months; and the ability to imitate adult behaviors in their brains months if not years before their bodies become actively involved, babies experience an unrivaled period of growth and opportunity during these first five years. Yet all these amazing feats and the many more that we will discuss don't just happen automatically. The research makes it ever clearer: what we do as parents and how we interact with our children during this time stands to considerably help (or hinder) their development.

The Early Bird Catches the Worm

WHEN IT COMES TO PAYING attention to children's development and how best to foster it, it's never too early to start. My professional focus on children, which has moved earlier and earlier over the past two decades, certainly reflects this belief. I've become increasingly convinced that many of the values that I—and all loving parents—care about most with respect to our children's futures take root in early childhood.

Even before I delved into all of the compelling neuroscience that supports why the brain is primed for learning essential life-long skills in early childhood, simply dealing with the practical challenges of raising young kids had me convinced that looking earlier is clearly the way to go. Take habits, for example. Given that habits are quite difficult to break, it proves only logical (not to mention most effective) for parents to encourage and establish healthy habits as early as possible, while anticipating and avoiding less desirable habits well before these have a chance to take hold. In both my pediatric practice and educational child care center, I have focused on helping hundreds if not thousands of parents tackle the day-to-day challenges of parenthood—from potty training and feeding to tooth brushing and sleeping—to trace them back to and address them at their roots. For example, if toddlers notoriously clamp their jaws shut and refuse to have their teeth brushed, then why not introduce a toothbrush in the first year, at an age when they happily put everything in their mouths? If some preschoolers are resistant to potty training because they fear the toilet flushing, why not be proactive and allow them as toddlers to accompany parents into the bathroom to do the honors so they grow accustomed to (supervised) flushing at an age when they're eager to do so and before fear has the chance to set in?

Well beyond these habit-focused examples are two compelling areas of research in early childhood development that I believe will leave you all the more convinced that earlier truly is better and enthusiastically setting your parenting sights on skill building beginning in the earliest weeks, months, and years of your child's life. The first area comprises a growing number of long-term studies that shed new light on just how predictive of children's future life successes the early presence of social-emotional and other key skills are. Equally convincing is a wealth of scientific evidence from brain research that now tells us—and shows us—about the toddler brain, including when and how key connections and skills develop. Just as today's top-performing companies recognize the importance of engaging employees from the minute they show up on the job, all of us in the business of raising children to become engaged, productive adults have the once-in-a-lifetime opportunity, through our earliest loving, caring, and nurturing interactions, to start shaping our children's brains and set them up for success from the day they're born.

Why *So* Early?

HAVING SPENT AS LONG AS I have in the parenting space both personally and professionally, I've learned to think carefully about not just what I want to say but also how it might be misconstrued. In this regard, I can't think of an easier target for misunderstanding or pushback than suggesting that all parents should follow a strategic plan that prescribes brain-building techniques designed specifically to help their toddlers get ahead in life. It's not lost on me that the notion of being more strategic about how we approach our babies and young children can sound cold, harsh, capitalistic, or even downright sacrilegious and may have some of you feeling a bit unsettled. In our culture, early childhood is, after all, generally regarded as sacred, a time when children should be cooed at, cuddled, and carefree. Well, the good news is that I couldn't agree more. Quite sensitive to these concerns myself, before I provide you with the insight and tools to start maximizing your child's potential, I think it's worth taking a moment to point out just what starting early is *not* about.

This book is *not* about creating baby geniuses—at least not in the traditional, academic sense of the word.[3] It is *not* about teaching babies to read before their first birthday, a concept that's been as decisively discredited as it has been marketed.[4,5] And it's most definitely *not* about pushing babies, toddlers, or preschoolers to master the many milestones of early childhood faster, earlier, or before it's developmentally appropriate. After all, the last I checked, nobody asks on a college or job application at what age you potty trained. Nor have I ever seen a study demonstrating any positive predictive value for precociously potty-trained infants with regard to their future life successes. This is, by the way, in contrast to the sorts of skills we will be focusing on—skills that naturally develop early when cultivated, and skills that parents can help build and strengthen during that critical window of opportunity defined by the first five years. As you'll see, these coveted social-emotional and executive function skills are proving to have a much longer-term impact on children's future lives than ditching diapers early.[6]

And, finally, this book is not advocating a forced march through parenthood; it's not recommending a tiger mom or dad approach for babies; it's not intended to put yet one more thing on your plate to add to any parenting guilt you may already experience; and it's not suggesting that the many issues hovering around helicopter parents should be put into action on the launch pad of babies' lives.

As strategic and intentional as this parenting "playbook" promises to be, with all of its supporting long-term studies, brain research and skill-building recommendations, it is actually meant to highlight and protect exactly what it is we consider to be so sacred about early childhood. It specifically presents the science- and brain-based evidence that supports, reinforces, and validates what many of us have always believed and acted on: that babies are meant to be held, cuddled, cooed at, and talked to—and nothing and no one is more important in this process than you!

One of the greatest connections I hope this book helps you and all parents make is to recognize just how powerfully important all of the fun, engaging, and nurturing activities you share with your children are for their future. As you step into your important role as both a caring, responsive adult and a brain builder, realize that, from the very beginning, this isn't about invading or contaminating early childhood. It's about capitalizing on your child's potential and the opportunity you have as a parent to help assemble the very same toolkit of skills today that your child will need tomorrow—in school, in work, and in life. And rather than having to sacrifice a precious moment of their early years to do it, you'll simply be able to appreciate them all the more.

What Happens in Early Childhood

IT HAS LONG BEEN SAID that children spend their first few years in school learning to read and the rest of their lives reading to learn. This simple yet poignant phrase helps capture the likely reality of why third-grade reading scores have long been considered predictive of all sorts of important life outcomes. The ability to read proficiently by the end of third grade has been tied to everything from high school graduation and future economic success to our country's global competitiveness and national security.[7]

With that in mind, would you like to know what is now thought to be a potential predictor of third-grade reading scores? A child's vocabulary at eighteen months of age. When I first heard this association presented several years back at a *business* conference, no less—ReadyNation's 2011 National Business Leader Summit on Early Childhood in Boston—it stopped me dead in my tracks. After all, at eighteen months, toddlers aren't even expected to be able to consistently string together two- to four-word sentences or to have mastered the names of familiar people or body parts yet—key developmental language milestones not typically achieved until the age of two.[8]

Think about what this means! If third-grade reading skills are used as a barometer to predict future life success, and researchers are now looking at toddlers' vocabularies as being predictive of third-grade reading scores, this reinforces just how pivotal early language development is. Remember, we're talking about language development that occurs long before children take their first steps, much less first set foot in kindergarten! This realization alone should serve as a hugely compelling reason why we can't afford to wait until our kids enter kindergarten, or even turn two, before we start building a strong foundation for their early language development and, in so doing, their future.

But there's more. New evidence of this reality comes from a study of nearly nine thousand US toddlers. Researchers at Penn State, University of California–Irvine, and Columbia University found that two-year-olds with larger vocabularies outperformed their peers with smaller vocabularies academically, of course, but also when it came to controlling their behaviors when they entered kindergarten three years later.[9] It's becoming increasingly clear that starting earlier is important for developing both vocabulary *and* other crucial lifelong skills, not the least of which are the social-emotional skills proved to be the bedrock for twenty-first-century success and well-being.

In my experiences as a parent, what has proven itself to be the most striking (and easily replicable) example of starting early grew out of my husband's and my commitment to read aloud to our children essentially from the day they were born. We had no formal reading lists nor any grand long-term read-aloud plans. Rather, what we did have, like just about all new parents, was a distinct lack of time and sleep—parental challenges exaggerated in our case by the fact that we both were spending long hours in the hospital completing our medical training when we became the tired but happy parents of three children in a period of only three-and-a-half years. Buried in our own day-to-day of clothing, crying, car seats, and diapers, carving out protected time to sit and read books with our kids seemed like an enjoyable, manageable, and worthwhile daily activity to which we could realistically aspire.

What started with board books and baby drool quickly progressed to picture books, shared "reading," and chapter books such that by the time our children were making their way through preschool, each of them could listen to stories for hours and still plead for more. Knowing all that I now know and am committed to sharing with you, I have come to see these years of shared reading time as not just a fun memory but as an activity that I believe had a profound impact on all three of my children.

As soon as they reached elementary school, I quickly realized that their noticeably early and impressive ability to focus and pay attention to both details and context helped them learn more, faster, and in greater detail than their peers. I can trace my younger son's love of nature, animals, and, most specifically, wolves back to a period when he was not yet three and we read the Julie of the Wolves series of chapter books; my older son's early and persistent command of the English language and love of reading has served him remarkably well through high school and beyond, even though he ultimately developed a strong preference for math and science.

What has, in hindsight, been clearly reinforced many times over is that all of the pages we turned, hours we spent, and bedtime stories we shared long before our children could read their first words or tie their first shoelaces were doing more than just building a collection of cherished memories. We were building critical connections.

On the Importance of Early Language Development

In our social world, the ability to communicate serves as a keystone to the mastery of all sorts of skills of lifelong value. Language has long been recognized as "the tool of the tools" by preeminent child development researchers, Lev Vygotsky among them, and as such, early language development has proven itself to be one of the most foundationally important skills of early childhood.

Learning to Play Nice

IN CONSIDERING JUST HOW BIG a potential role nurturing certain early skills plays in improving children's lives, a compelling study published in 2015 in the *American Journal of Public Health* ventured beyond vocabulary, self-control, and ingenuity to get at the heart of what every parent hopes to foster, not to mention what every employer hopes to find in his or her employees: the ability to play nice.[10] This representative social competency study began in the early 1990s. Kindergarten teachers across the United States rated the degree to which more than 750 students exhibited pro-social behaviors such as sharing, cooperating, listening, and helping others. Researchers followed up with these children over the next twenty years and found that the higher the children had scored on their social skills at age five, the better their adult outcomes were across an impressively wide range of areas that included education, employment, substance use, and mental health. Those with higher scores in kindergarten were more likely to graduate from high school, attain a college degree in early adulthood, and have full-time employment at age twenty-five. Those kindergartners with lower scores, on the other hand, were more likely to have been arrested, recently used marijuana, and live in public housing.

Putting Marshmallows to the Test

STRONG SOCIAL SKILLS DEVELOPED IN the first five years are not the only things with predictive value. So, too, are marshmallows. Now, I have to say that, as a pediatrician committed first and foremost to keeping children safe, my initial reaction to marshmallows in the context of young children used to be alarm about their potential choking risk. Because I am firmly committed to promoting healthy eating habits, a close second was concern about their excessive sugar content. Nowadays, however, I find myself discussing marshmallows for very different reasons.

So, what do marshmallows have to do with early childhood beyond posing a choking hazard and playing a substantive role in the construction of s'mores? The answer can be traced to not one but two different tests that, by making good use of marshmallows, help us better understand the implications of twenty-first-century skill development during our children's earliest years.

In the first instance, which we will discuss in greater detail in Chapter 4, landmark research first conducted at Stanford University[11] reveals that how well a preschooler can resist the temptation to eat a marshmallow tells us a lot more than you might imagine about his or her future abilities, achievements, and outcomes, including everything from SAT scores to body mass index (BMI).

In the other study, on which I elaborate in Chapter 9, an intriguing design challenge using marshmallows reveals that young children routinely surpass their highly trained and corporate-level adult challengers in their abilities to collaborate, iterate, innovate, and exercise creativity.[12]

In both instances, the skills the young participants demonstrate represent the very same twenty-first-century skills so highly coveted in the adult world. Not only do marshmallows serve to focus much-needed attention on the predictive value of skills such as delayed gratification, adaptability, and perseverance, but the Corporate Marshmallow Challenge also offers us a humbling reminder that even highly educated adults can learn a thing or two from young children's ability to inquire, explore, and think creatively about the world. All told, these two marshmallow "tests" shed light on important aspects of early childhood and provide information more pertinent to and predictive of future life success than a child's IQ score ever could.

From toddler vocabulary to marshmallow mastery to kindergarten-ready social skills, each study and many more tell us, in no uncertain terms, that early really does make a difference. As we come to recognize the importance of social-emotional, "non-cognitive," and other life skills, we also need to recognize that what happens in early childhood doesn't *stay* in early childhood. Rather, the early presence and development of these skills stand to play a significant role in determining our children's future health, educational, professional, and life trajectories. In other words, they stand to determine both our children's overall well-being and realization of our ultimate parenting goals.

From Social Skills to Toddler Brains: Making the Connections

AS WE SET OUR PARENTING sights on how best to nurture our children's skills early, we are no longer limited to simply observing how these skills manifest in outward, easily recognizable ways. From speaking and reading to understanding and playing nice with others, the past decade's worth of baby brain research has yielded amazing results. Armed with new technologies and new insights, we now have the ability to not only identify relevant areas and attributes of the developing brain but also determine what we as parents can actually do—right down to the level of connecting neurons—to help bring these skills to life.

The best way to appreciate your toddler's brain is as a dynamic work in progress. Sure, babies are born with just about all of the brain cells they'll need throughout their lives, but just like young children, these cells have a lot of work to do when it comes to the important tasks of learning to communicate and collaborate with each other. What makes the first few years of brain development so dynamic is the fact that all hundred billion or so neurons (a number said to rival the number of planets in the Milky Way![13]) quickly begin connecting with each other at a mind-expanding rate of up to seven hundred new neural connections (or *synapses*) per second. As a result, 85 percent of brain growth is believed to occur within the first three years.

First to rise to the challenge is the basic brain circuitry for vision and hearing, which starts forming right after birth. The neural networks that serve as the foundation for language development follow soon thereafter and are generally established within the first year. As for the coming together of neurons responsible for the "higher" cognitive functions—thinking, reasoning, and communicating—that make up the building blocks of the coveted twenty-first-century toolkit, they are largely in place by around age five. It is during these early years of very rapid brain growth that particularly sensitive periods for learning and development occur and are now recognized as exceptionally influential in shaping the toddler brain.[14]

In a world where connections matter, it's important to understand, however, that it's not simply a matter of "he or she with the *most* connections wins." Rather, a young child's developing brain is more like a "use it or lose it" machine, ready from day one to strengthen neural pathways that are repeatedly put to good use while pruning away connections that aren't. It's the *strength* of these early connections that really matters.

What strengthens these neural connections? The answer is deceptively simple: it's us. All of the early, everyday experiences we share with our children serve as the key ingredients necessary to effectively build and strengthen their neural networks, their brains, and ultimately the toolkit of skills they'll need to succeed. Our understanding of how we can influence this early, dynamic, brain-building process represents a fundamentally important shift in our parental thinking. It also provides an actionable plan for accomplishing our parenting objective of setting our children up for success.

The Amazing Baby Brain: What's Going On in There?

AS WE DISCUSSED IN WHY NOW, modern technology has advanced just about every facet of modern life. Brain imaging is no exception. Instead of watching and waiting patiently until children babble, toddle, walk, or talk to get an outward glimpse of what's going on beneath the surface, improved imaging technologies that measure everything from blood flow and light absorption to oxygen consumption and electrical activity have enabled us to peer inside babies' brains in ways we never could before.[15]

One of the newest and most fascinating modern advancements in baby brain imaging is a cutting-edge technology called MEG (*magnetoencephalography*). There are only a handful of MEG machines in the United States, with only one, at the time of this writing, located at the University of Washington's Institute for Learning and Brain Sciences (I-LABS) in Seattle that is specifically set up to be used with infants. The machine fits over a baby's head in a way that the Institute's codirector describes as resembling a space-age salon hair dryer. This silent and noninvasive technology detects magnetic fields naturally produced by electrical currents in the brain, thus allowing research scientists the unprecedented ability to visualize the real-time activity of the billions of neurons and trillions of neural connections in very young children's brains as they think their baby thoughts and go about their baby business interacting with and responding to their parents. As you can imagine, the results are both intriguing and informative, helping to shed new light on everything from the development of language and problem-solving ability to that of social and emotional understanding.

The Power of Social Networking

MEG, ALONG WITH OTHER NEW baby brain research techniques, provides some of the first tangible brain-based data to support the fact that our day-to-day social interactions with our babies are key to their learning and brain development. When you talk to your baby while changing a diaper, sing songs while playing, lovingly respond to cries, and take a walk outside and point out what you see, you're doing so much more than just checking to-do's off of your daily parenting list. You're actually flipping a switch, firing up your child's learning, and using the power of social interactions to create strong and valuable neural networks.

As an example of how researchers are putting this point to the test, world-renowned baby brain and language researcher and I-LABS codirector Dr. Patricia Kuhl conducted a landmark study in which a group of nine- and ten-month-old infants were exposed to the Mandarin language for the first time.[16] For some, this involved sitting in a room with a native Mandarin speaker who played with toys and read children's books to them while speaking in Mandarin. Other infants watched on DVD (rather than interacting in person) as Mandarin-speaking adults similarly played with the toys and read books. A third group of babies listened to an audio-only version of the interaction, without any accompanying images or social interaction.

After the babies participated in a dozen of these twenty-five-minute sessions over the course of a month or so, something striking occurred. Although neither the babies who watched the DVD nor those who listened to the audio showed any improvement in their ability to distinguish phonetic elements specific to the Mandarin language, those who had heard Mandarin while *socially* interacting with the person speaking did. In fact, they showed remarkable learning despite less than five cumulative hours of exposure to the foreign language. Not only did they do significantly better than the other babies but their skills were actually found to be on par with those of ten-month-old Taiwanese infants who'd heard their native language since birth.

As a prime example of the latest in baby-babble-meets-neuroscience research, Kuhl's study makes clear that social interaction is an inherently important aspect of language learning. This, along with other detailed research on how babies' brains activate and respond to interactions with adults, has led Kuhl to propose a theory that should be of profound significance to each and every one of us: babies' brains are socially gated.[17] What this theory suggests is that the key to unlocking our children's tremendous early learning potential, all the way down to the level of activating, connecting, and fine-tuning their brain circuitry, is deeply dependent on our social interactions with them.

Investigating the Baby Brain

In her TEDx talk called "The Linguistic Genius of Babies," researcher Dr. Patricia Kuhl stated: "We are embarking on a grand and golden age of knowledge about child[ren]'s brain development. We're going to be able to see a child's brain as they experience an emotion, as they learn to speak and read, as they solve a math problem, as they have an idea. . . . In investigating the child's brain, we're going to uncover deep truths about what it means to be human, and in the process, we may be able to help keep our own minds open to learning for our entire lives."

A Game of Serve and Return

IN PRACTICAL TERMS, THIS MEANS that all of our day-to-day, back-and-forth interactions with our children in the earliest days, months, and years of their lives literally help to shape their brain architecture. Researchers at Harvard's Center on the Developing Child describe this recipe for brain-building success, using tennis terminology, as "serve and return."[18] To help you gain a better sense of what these tennis-volley-like serve-and-return interactions are all about, just picture a young infant. He spontaneously smiles. You respond by smiling back. Keenly attuned to your reaction, he and his developing neural connections take your smile as positive feedback, and before you know it, you come face to face with one of the most eagerly anticipated developmental milestones of two- and three-month-olds: the social smile.

Now think about cooing. He coos, you coo, and this seemingly simple serve-and-return interaction, along with all of the many daily, back-and-forth interactions you share with your baby, literally lays the social and neuronal networks for future language and communication.

Early Executive Functions

NO DISCUSSION OF STRATEGIC EARLY childhood skill building would be complete without shifting gears and directing our attention to an area of the brain known as the *prefrontal cortex*. The prefrontal cortex makes up the front third of the brain, but, more importantly, it serves as home to a core group of skills known as *executive function skills*.[19] Although the "executive" description fittingly brings to mind intellect, organizational skills, operational expertise, and focus, today's executives must also possess social and emotional intelligence. In this regard, it is worth pointing out that executive function skills are also what enable the brain to integrate our intellectual thoughts *and* our feelings and emotions.

Technically speaking, executive function skills are defined by three core abilities:

1. **Inhibitory (or impulse) control:** The ability to control our impulses. This skill allows us to think before we act, resist temptations (not to mention distractions and habits), and prioritize our actions rather than acting purely impulsively. It's what helps us "bite our tongues," control our emotions, wait our turn, and keep from daydreaming when we need to focus.

2. **Working memory:** The ability to keep lots of different pieces of information in mind and accessible. Clearly instrumental in the completion of just about any task, working memory has been described as the mental surface on which we can place important information so that it is ready to use in the course of our everyday lives.[20]

3. **Cognitive or mental flexibility:** The ability to quickly shift our attention and switch mental gears when faced with new information, circumstances, perspectives, or priorities. Cognitive flexibility also allows out-of-the-box thinking—allowing us to apply different rules to different circumstances and to keep our thinking from becoming too rigid and ourselves from becoming too set in our ways.

Perhaps the best way to think of the executive function skills collectively is as described by Harvard's Center on the Developing Child: they are the "air traffic control system" of our brain.[21] After all, as center director Dr. Jack Shonkoff explains, our executive function skills make it possible for us to focus, filter distractions, and switch mental gears as we juggle, organize, integrate, and manage multiple pieces of information at the same time.

> ### EFs: As Important as the ABCs
>
> Executive function skills, sometimes referred to by researchers in the world of child development as "EFs," are proving themselves to be more strongly associated with school readiness than traditional measures such as IQ, math skills, or even the ABCs of entry-level reading.[22]

Now think back for a moment to the skills we discussed in WHY NOW as being essential for success in the twenty-first century. The connection between these real-world skills and their brain-based counterparts suddenly becomes quite evident: when we talk about the world shifting from being purely IQ-driven to one that requires us to integrate our intellectual capabilities with our social-emotional skills, we're also talking about the brain's ability to integrate these two elements. In other words, we're talking about the need for strong executive functions. When we talk about the complex, rapidly changing world and how it demands individual agility and adaptability, we're also talking about the analogous *cognitive* flexibility that allows the brain to rapidly and seamlessly jump between mental tasks. This, too, is an executive function. And when we talk about living in an Information Age that requires us to focus our attention and filter information in the face of an endless barrage of details and distractions, not to mention integrate new information and put it into context with what we already know, once again, we're talking about executive functions.

In short, anyone who cares about nurturing skills today that their children will need tomorrow needs to attend to executive function skills, and they need to do so early. Although babies aren't born with executive function skills, we now know that these skills start developing shortly after birth and go through a significant growth spurt during the preschool years. Sure, these skills don't develop to their fullest extent until around age twenty-five, but the period between the ages of three and five years provides us with an unrivaled and much earlier window of opportunity for influencing dramatic growth.[23]

And, like all parts of the brain, the more that executive function skills are exercised, the stronger they become. So, how can you nurture them? The National Scientific Council on the Developing Child sums it up best: healthy, caring relationships along with engaging and stimulating experiences are literally food for a child's growing brain.[24]

Baby Brain Games

CONSIDERED TOGETHER IN THE CONTEXT of your child's developing brain, concepts such as socially gated learning, serve-and-return interactions, and executive functioning represent and highlight just how crucial our role is in our children's early learning, skill development, and future. The evidence is now abundantly clear: babies are born with incredible capabilities and potential. Both the timing and the quality of their earliest experiences and interactions with the people they trust most, as well as the environment in which they experience the world around them, all help to shape the architecture of their developing brains.

Even before we had the benefit of all that modern-day neuroscience now offers us, eminent psychologist Lev Vygotsky was prescient in recognizing that "it is through others that we become ourselves." In parenting terms, all of the talking, cooing, singing, hugging, reading, playing, and exploring the world that you do with your baby matters a whole lot to who they will ultimately become.

Summing Up the Surprising Science

NOW, BEFORE WE JUMP RIGHT in to the rest of the book's promised focus on skills and skill building, it's worth reminding ourselves that a lot of what we tend to do, feel, and believe about how best to raise our children has been handed down for generations, shared among friends and neighbors, and passed along via the networks that make up today's social media channels. Although these early parenting social support systems have the potential to play an important role, it's not always easy to tell the extent to which any sort of research or evidence bears out all of this well-intentioned advice.

At the same time, it is also understandable (but nevertheless misguided) to assume that knowledge about early child development is static. Whereas the routine developmental milestones of early childhood admittedly have been spelled out for decades— by pediatricians, the Centers for Disease Control and Prevention (CDC),[25] and many others—a growing body of surprising new science about your child's earliest social, emotional, and cognitive development is simply not to be missed. The more aware you are of the dynamic process of baby brain growth and how best to apply all of the evidence of early opportunity that comes with it, the more you can tailor what you do to facilitate the making of these connections and your expectations of your child's budding abilities.

Although it is typically the stuff of which modern-day pediatric and child development textbooks are made, I wanted to offer you the following "so-what" overview of this exciting science so that you can keep it in mind as you read the rest of this book. It is my hope that you will also use these takeaways as your parenting North Star of sorts as you get down to the oh-so-important business of raising your child to ultimately become a happy, healthy, and productive adult.

Here are some of the more intriguing things we now know to be true about children from birth to age five. They are:

1. **Citizens of the world:** In a world of global interconnectedness, it's clear that preparing our children for success now more than ever involves preparing them to think globally. That may seem like a very tall order to add to our new parenting to-do list, but it turns out that nature has given us, and babies, a head start. Through landmark research done by Dr. Patricia Kuhl and others, we know that babies can, at birth, recognize the sounds of *all* of the world's languages—a skill that has earned them admiring recognition as true "citizens of the world" but that also fades over the first year in the absence of ongoing cultivation.[26]

2. **Socially gated learners:** Though we like to think of young children as sponges—able to absorb everything about the world around them—research tells us otherwise, as does prominent University of Southern California neuroscience researcher Pat Levitt.[27] Whereas sponges absorb anything and everything from their surroundings, Levitt points out, babies in fact do not . . . unless, that is, the proper conditions are met. What are those research-proven prerequisite conditions? Social, human interaction and connectedness.

3. **Followers of the rules of engagement:** In an era when everyone from educators to employers are recognizing the importance of engagement and its impact on learning and productivity, the science of child development is simultaneously and convincingly demonstrating that even very young children also seem to play

by strikingly similar rules of engagement. As but one of many examples, toddlers and preschoolers demonstrate increased learning when they are taught by someone (in person or even a character/person onscreen) who actively engages them by speaking directly to them, using their name, and asking them direct questions.[28, 29]

4. **Emotion detectors:** At the same time that the term *emotional intelligence* is being recognized as two of the hottest words in corporate America and deemed fundamental to early and life-long learning,[30] a burgeoning field of empathy research shows that very young children, even those yet to celebrate their first birthday, are already remarkably astute at picking up on and responding to the emotions of those around them and are able to do so months (if not years) before this affective skill becomes outwardly apparent.

5. **Face-time followers:** Given that a whole lot of twenty-first-century-relevant information can be gleaned from peoples' faces—not the least of which are others' emotions, thoughts, and intentions—it is of no small significance that research shows that infants as young as newborns prefer to pay attention to faces (both representations of faces and real ones). This face-following skill improves significantly over the first year of life.[31]

6. **Precocious cryptographers:** From babbling at six months to speaking in complete sentences by the age of three, infants master language in a rapid, predictable, and deceptively simple way. Yet, though this universally early human ability to "crack the speech code"[32] may understandably be perceived as child's play, make no mistake about it: it actually represents an incredible cognitive and cryptographic feat of significant scope and import, not to mention one that has yet to be solved by adults or our computers *or* our advances in AI (artificial intelligence).

7. **Repeat performers:** Although repetition-weary parents may, on occasion, question the value of reading aloud the same book over and over and *over* again, when it comes to young children's ability to learn, the benefits of repetition are measurable.[33,34] Interestingly, the repetition effect may help improve children's ability to learn from video content as well; studies have shown that toddlers can perform a task they have witnessed an adult doing multiple times on video nearly as well as those who had the benefit of a single, face-to-face demonstration of the same task.[35] Yes, social, in-person interactions matter, but repetition has its benefits no matter what format.

8. **Musical maestros:** Okay, so "maestro" may be a bit strong, but research that suggests music has the potential to boost broader cognitive skills and enhance children's abilities to detect, expect, and quickly react to patterns in the world around them should come as music to your ears. In a first-of-its-kind study, babies exposed to particular rhythmic patterns in music were subsequently able to detect the same underlying rhythm not only in new music, as might be expected, but also in spoken language![36] State-of-the-art neuroimaging provides even greater insights into the potential effects of a baby's brain on music, revealing that the auditory cortex is not the only region of the brain that is actively engaged. Also activated is the prefrontal cortex, the very same part of the brain responsible for executive function skills so critically important for controlling attention and detecting patterns.

9. **Skilled statisticians:**[37] In today's data-driven, technology-informed world, mastering the ability to mine and classify information and make predictions based on real-world data sounds like a surefire way to land a great job in Silicon Valley. In the world of baby brain development, however, it also happens to accurately describe how babies as young as eight months old apply statistics to learn new words,[38] how fourteen-month-olds

can generalize and classify objects,[39] and how two-and-a-half-year-olds can predict cause and effect. Although the studies that produce this evidence are often cute and colorful—involving bright balls pulled out of boxes, made-up words, and fanciful toy machines—the behind-the-scenes statistical skills they help to illuminate are surprisingly complex.

10. **Inherent innovators:** Our continually improving understanding of the toddler brain tells us that what young children lack in valued "adult" abilities, such as long-term planning and other executive function–dependent skills that take time to develop, they make up for in their natural-born ability to imagine, create, iterate, and innovate. The challenge for us, as parents, is to help them foster the former without squelching the latter.

Getting Down to Business

KNOWING THAT BABIES' BRAINS ARE at their most flexible and growing more rapidly in early childhood than at any other time in life provides you, the innovative parent, with evidence-based windows of opportunity to serve as Chief Architect of your baby's brain, committed to strengthening the neural connections that will become your child's lifelong pathways to success. As you connect what you do with your child now to the enduring neural connections you're helping build, your parenting role will take on even greater significance than you may ever have imagined. So, if you didn't already consider your job as Primary Role Model, First Teacher, Ultimate Leader, and Chief Engagement Officer to be important enough, you can now officially add Master Brain Builder to that list.

And, with that, let the brain games begin—and may the Force be with you!

PART 2

QI Skills

NOW THAT WE'VE TAKEN THE time to get a feel for the direction the world is heading, get up to speed on the latest in baby brain science, and commit to thinking strategically about our parenting role, I hope you're convinced now more than ever of just what an exciting opportunity you have to build your baby's brain and foster foundational skills that your child will undoubtedly put to good use for a lifetime. After all, the surprising science that supports your child's earliest development is proving to be one and the same as the science that has caught the attention of everyone from business leaders to bankers, happiness and well-being experts to educators, administrators and even the Federal Reserve, economists, and others focused on workforce development. The most obvious next step is thus to roll up our sleeves and focus our attention and efforts on the well-defined list of twenty-first-century skills for success.

As you'll recall from WHY NOW, this list of skills has changed considerably from the predominantly academic, cognitive, fact-based, and IQ-focused abilities of days past. Now included on the list are traits and abilities like *creativity, curiosity, communication, collaboration,* and *critical thinking.* In addition to these all-important "five Cs," a fourth R has been added to the traditional "three Rs" of reading, 'riting, and 'rithmetic to elevate the importance of *relationships.* And, of course, there's *empathy, adaptability,* and the *ability to fail.*

At the core of this alphabet-soup-like list of coveted abilities are a host of crucial skills variously referred to as *emotional intelligence, social-emotional skills, executive function skills, grit, perseverance, non-cognitive skills, soft skills,* and even *character, people skills,* and *life skills.* What this unwieldy list adds up to is a category of clearly identified, highly valued, frequently discussed, and increasingly researched abilities that start to develop early in life and, up until this point, have lacked a distinctive, collective, and descriptive name.

Given just how important we know them to be, it strikes me as odd that we don't have something suitable to call them. Though they do, in fact, serve as a complementary skill set to IQ, simply continuing to refer to them as "non-IQ" or "other" skills doesn't seem right, as it does very little to signify their importance. Neither, I would argue, does calling them "soft" or "non-cognitive," since neither description conveys anything close to these skills' grounding in brain science, much less their significant value.

Convinced of the need for a name to call these key skills, I began my search for a better, more concise, and appropriate way to describe them. After quite some time, I happened upon a word that perfectly encapsulates these so-called other and non-IQ skills. That word is QI (pronounced "key").

The first time I was introduced to the word QI, I admit I had to ask what it meant (and how to pronounce it). The thought-provoking answer came in the form of a question: "Do you know the phrase, 'May the Force be with you!' from *Star Wars*? QI represents that force." In a world where first impressions matter, QI's fundamental representation of a positive—not to mention immensely well-recognized and distinctly popular—life force seemed fitting for my usage, even if not entirely synonymous with *Star Wars'* Force. After all, there's no question that the collective skills we're talking about represent a powerful force in our children's lives. The fact that the word sounds like "key" made it even better, because any mistaking of the two words would still convey just how foundationally important—or key—these skills really are.

In digging deeper, I soon discovered quite a lot more reinforcing information about QI. As a concept describing the flow of energy that sustains human beings, QI has long been synonymous with life force, well before it reached pop culture fame. QI is thought to permeate all living things and link elements together, and it is believed to be both something we're born with (*yuan qi*[1]) and something we can cultivate, develop, and learn—a characteristic that fits with what you'll soon discover is true of each of the skills we'll discuss. And although QI has commonly been associated with traditional Chinese culture, concepts very similar to QI as a positive or vital life force have also long been recognized across centuries and cultures, from Hindu, ancient Greek, and Hawaiian to Tibetan, Buddhist, and Hebrew. For anyone searching for the best way to describe a set of universal life skills, QI as "the life-process or flow of energy that sustains living beings"[2] definitely seems to fit the bill.

It's worth noting that the pairing of the letters Q and I also has a well-established use in healthcare and other systems, where QI is commonly understood to represent quality improvement. In this context, QI describes a variety of formal approaches to the analysis of performance and systematic efforts to improve it.[3] Although there are multiple models for QI in this regard (FADE [Focus, Analyze, Develop, Execute, Evaluate], PDSA [Plan, Do, Study, Act], CQI [Continuous Quality Improvement], and Six Sigma, to name a few), they all have in common a clear-cut goal of improvement and supporting ongoing efforts to advance quality—additional aspects of QI that fit particularly well with our purposes, given the role that fostering of the non-IQ skills stands to play in continually improving the quality of our children's lives.

And, finally, as if its meaning alone didn't make QI a good fit, the word QI serves as a perfect complement to IQ—literally! They may share the same letters, but they represent two different and complementary skill sets. IQ is all about cognition in a more concrete, fact-based, academic sense. IQ includes the traditional three Rs, for example. People with high IQs have long been viewed as book smart and gifted with numbers, words, and patterns. They memorize, analyze, and take tests well. Yet, as we've discussed in WHY NOW and WHY EARLY, high IQ alone is not enough to thrive in the twenty-first-century landscape. Not that it has ceased to be important, but rather we now recognize that something beyond IQ is needed to ensure that our children are well equipped to connect with others and successfully interact with the complex world around them.

Having found a word that represents a positive life force recognized for centuries and across cultures, a word that conveniently sounds like key and serves as a complement to IQ, a word that even when mistaken to mean quality improvement still describes the emerging twenty-first-century skills we have the opportunity to nurture and strengthen in the earliest years of our children's lives, allow me to present what I propose we call QI Skills. Divided into easy-to-understand, parent- and kid-friendly categories, the following is a brief description of each of the seven QI Skills.

1. **ME:** Self-management skills that include self-awareness, self-regulation, self-control, attention, and focus.
2. **WE:** The people skills that allow us to understand, share, and play well with others, including the language, empathy, listening, and social-emotional skills necessary for effective communication, collaboration, and teamwork.
3. **WHY:** Skills that include questioning, curiosity, and inquisitiveness. These allow us to see the world as a question mark and to strive for a better understanding of how the world works.
4. **WILL:** Self-motivation and drive define these critically important skills.
5. **WIGGLE:** Physical *and* intellectual restlessness make up the WIGGLE Skills that play a key role in putting WHY and WILL into action.
6. **WOBBLE:** Skills that allow for, build, and foster agility, adaptability, and resilience and that confer the ability to face, overcome, and learn from failure.
7. **WHAT IF:** Skills that encompass curiosity, imagination, and creativity and ultimately allow us to not just understand how the world is but also envision how it could be.

In each of the following seven chapters, I focus on a given QI Skill, elaborating on what defines it and why it's so important for success and achievement in the twenty-first century, and then I trace it back to its early childhood origins. We'll also take a close look at how to recognize and nurture each skill and boost brain development during the critically significant first five years of your child's life. I draw from the latest in neuroscience research to stories from my own experiences to examples demonstrating just how valued each given skill is in today's world—in school, in business, and in life.

At the end of each chapter, I provide plenty of age-appropriate activities and strategies you can apply in your day-to-day parenting life. You'll notice that many of these are activities that parents have used for countless generations, such as talking, reading, cooing, singing songs, playing games, and more. What sets these activities apart, however, is that now you can approach them with a brand-new mindset of brain building and fostering QI Skill development. My hope is that you'll also feel inspired to think up new ones using the strategic-plan approach of engaging with your child in an intentional way in order to lay the foundation for twenty-first-century success. By understanding these trusted and effective parenting activities in their QI Skill context, it is my sincere hope that you'll find yourself not only more motivated, engaged, and committed to purposefully fostering your child's QI Skills but also truly empowered as you embrace and enjoy the experience of doing so!

Let's start with ME.

QI Skill 1

ME

Focusing Attention on Self-Management

He that controls others may be powerful
But he who has mastered himself is mightier still.

—Lao Tzu

DESPITE ITS SEEMINGLY NEWFOUND POPULARITY, the catchphrase "Keep Calm and Carry On" has been traced back as far as the late 1930s, just prior to the start of World War II.[1] The British government printed this motivational saying on millions of posters intended to boost the morale of British citizens faced with impending attack. Fast-forward to today, and this catchy phrase and its accompanying crown have become an impressively popular modern-day meme, commercialized, printed, and even parodied on baseball caps, T-shirts, posters, coffee mugs, and all sorts of other memorabilia. With relevance spanning decades as well as cultures and continents, it's worth considering just what about these five words generates such historical and modern pop culture interest. I believe the answer lies in our instinctive awareness of just how valuable it is to be in control of our thoughts, feelings, and actions in order to focus and get things done. It is this fundamentally important ability, as well as a whole host of related keep-calm abilities, that captures the essence of the first QI Skill: ME.

All About Me

AS A TODDLER, MY SON wore a T-shirt featuring a disproportionately large stick figure standing on a very small earth with planets orbiting around it and a large, bold arrow pointing to the figure. A caption proclaimed, "Me: The center of the universe!" At the time, I thought the T-shirt was cute—and an accurate representation of most two-year-olds' worldview. The problem is, for some children today, this view seems to continue well beyond the early years, raising the question of whether they are growing up with too much of a sense of "me" for their own good.

If considered in this light, some might argue that rather than warranting the designation of a skill, this me-as-center-of-the-universe mentality represents instead a concerning attitude of entitlement. One might even conclude that this me-centric notion actually represents what's wrong with how we're raising the next generation. Although I share this concern regarding the pervasive selfie-centered view rendered on my toddler son's T-shirt, this image of "me" in no way captures the ME Skills we will discuss in this chapter. Rather, ME Skills represent a set of skills that will, in fact, serve as a key to your child's future life success, not to mention as the foundation for the development of all other QI Skills.

So, what, exactly, are ME Skills? ME Skills are best described as *self-management* skills. Breaking this first set of QI Skills down into its component parts, they involve the following:

- Self-awareness
- Self-control
- Self-regulation

In addition, ME Skills include such abilities as inner focus, mindfulness, and aspects of emotional intelligence such as being in touch with oneself and one's emotions. Also at the heart of ME Skills are the executive function skills introduced in WHY EARLY—those brain-based skills that start developing surprisingly early in life and ultimately allow us to manage, regulate, and control our emotions and behavior, not to mention the underlying cognitive processes responsible for reasoning, planning, and problem solving.

That's what we're aiming for. In young children, however, ME Skills often look quite different while they're still developing. So, how might we translate ME to the world of toddlers and preschoolers? Quite straightforwardly: a good self-management day in the life of a toddler can be defined as a day in which no one bites his or her friends. In fact, when you stop to think about it, what so many of the commonly used phrases of toddlerhood such as "Keep your hands to yourself!" "Sit still!" "Wait your turn!" and "Don't bite your friends!" are asking of young children is that they learn to employ their newly emerging self-control and impulse control skills in ways that two-, three-, and four-year-olds experience them.

When we think about what ME Skills look like in young children, one of the most striking realizations is their notable absence in the first few years. That's because impulsive behavior naturally dominates until the executive functions, focus and attention as well as impulse control, start to kick in around age three. Therefore, the purpose of this chapter is to help you better focus your attention on this set of ME-focused skills and understand when and how best to help your child build a strong and early foundation right when your child's brain is developing the capacity to exercise them.

Why Me?

FROM THE WORLD OF BOARD books to boardrooms, the value of ME Skills is readily apparent. Society today clearly values level-headedness and the abilities to pay attention, stay focused, manage one's emotions, "keep calm and carry on," and keep one's cool even when everyone else is losing theirs. Self-control and self-regulation are essential for getting there. Although ME Skills are hardly a new concept, what is new is our recognition of just how important they are to twenty-first-century success and the development of other QI Skills. In addition, we're learning more about just how early the foundational building blocks for ME Skills begin to take shape. Before considering the latter, let's first take a look at the big-picture, modern-day case for how self-management has emerged as a critical twenty-first-century business competency.

In the Business of Me:
From Business to Personal Management

AS A FAMED MANAGEMENT CONSULTANT, educator, and prolific author, Peter Drucker has often been referred to as the "Master of Management." Considered one of if not the most influential business management thinkers of the twentieth century,[2] he has been credited with coining the term "knowledge worker," foreseeing the rise of the nonprofit sector, and being one of the first to stress the importance of the customer in business strategy.[3] In the words of *Good to Great* author Jim Collins, "Drucker's primary contribution is not a single idea, but rather an entire body of work that has one gigantic advantage: nearly all of it is essentially right."[4]

In other words, it's safe to say that Drucker's ideas have had a tremendous impact on shaping business as we know it today. With such an impressive track record of valuable insights, it was of no small significance when Drucker's focus took a distinct turn near the end of his career as he looked toward the twenty-first century and what it might have in store. Increasingly convinced that "success in the knowledge economy [will come] to those who know themselves—their strengths, their values, and how they best perform," Drucker recognized the need to manage ourselves as creating "a revolution in human affairs." As Daniel Pink so clearly summarized in his book, *Drive: The Surprising Truth About What Motivates Us*, "Although he's best known for his thoughts on managing businesses, toward the end of his career Drucker signaled the next frontier: *self-management*."[5] What he left the business world and, I believe, the parenting world with was a particularly noteworthy insight: knowledge of oneself, accompanied by the ability to manage oneself, is absolutely critical for both work and life success.

With all eyes shifting to self-management, it raises the question: Why? The answer is fairly intuitive once you think it through. People who are adept at self-management get things done. They execute their objectives rather than talk a good game. It doesn't matter whether you work in a software company, at a hospital, or at home. Distractions abound in every field. As a result, it can be difficult to achieve objectives, meet deadlines, and operate efficiently and effectively. People who are skilled at self-management—who can focus on the job at hand, who don't get sidetracked, and who accomplish their tasks quickly and creatively—are of great value, no matter where they work or what they do.

Remaining calm and in control of one's emotions can also be a challenge in today's world and workplace. Emotions can run high in all types of environments, whether due to increased stress, tight deadlines, or short-tempered or demanding colleagues. People are being asked to work in diverse team structures more now than ever before. As a result, the increased likelihood of having to work with someone who has a different skill set or who comes from a different background can prove difficult. Conflicts can occur, and being able to self-manage in these circumstances is a great advantage, both for an individual's career and for the organization where he or she works.

Putting Mindfulness to Work

NOW CONSIDER MINDFULNESS, A PRACTICE that has been prominently making its way into public and corporate consciousness. At first glance, a business-focused discussion may seem like an odd place to mention mindfulness. After all, for many, the word itself may conjure images of zenned-out yogis and uber-disciplined monks. But, as someone who's taken a total of one yoga class in her life and who has yet to perch on a meditation pillow, I'm not suggesting that at all. Instead, consider for a moment the definition of mindfulness: a mental state achieved by focusing one's awareness on the present moment while calmly acknowledging and accepting one's feelings, thoughts, and bodily sensations. That's precisely what ME Skills achieve. Given that self-awareness, self-control, and self-regulation are all recognized as crucial aspects of self-management, the practice of mindfulness is becoming an increasingly important component of exercising and mastering ME Skills in the workplace.

Practicing mindfulness, as it turns out, can be as simple as sitting quietly and focusing on your breath for a couple of minutes, which is something you can do at your desk, in your car, or on a crowded subway—no incense required. Simple though it may seem, the payoffs are proving themselves to be well worth it. Mindfulness techniques have been shown to improve cognitive functioning and decision making for adults and even, as you'll soon find out, for preschoolers. It only stands to reason that corporate mindfulness programs, able to yield these sorts of desirable results, are springing up in the most unlikely places—from workplaces to airports (with yoga and meditation rooms reportedly available for Zen-on-the-go at the San Francisco, Dallas, Raleigh, Burlington, Vermont, and Chicago airports![6]). And, yes, mindfulness training is even starting to make its way into our preschool classrooms.

Before we get to the potential of teaching mindfulness to preschoolers, however, let me first share a couple of specific examples of self-management training in the form of mindfulness programs that currently exist at some of today's leading businesses. For example, Google's head of People Operations Laszlo Bock describes in his book *Work Rules!* how science-based mindfulness is woven into the corporate culture of Google, which boasts an actual mindfulness team run by a Google engineer-turned-mindfulness-guru named Bill Duane.[7] Duane explains that business is simply a machine made out of people, and mindfulness serves as the WD-40 for the company, lubricating the sticky spots among its many working parts (in Duane's case, those parts consist of driven Googlers).

This new corporate embrace of mindfulness isn't limited to the likes of Google. SAP, the world's largest business software company, also employs the science of self-awareness and the power of mindfulness, as evidenced by a dedicated mindfulness programs director who recognizes that "once you know yourself, you will manage yourself better," and a chief learning officer, who reportedly incorporated mindfulness into the SAP curriculum to help the company's hundreds of thousands of employees become better workers.[8] In other words, in the contemporary world of work, the ability to pay attention without distraction and to pause and get centered before reacting is of significant value. As you're about to find out, this and the other key ME Skills start developing long before your child lands her first job.

Self-Management: The *Early* Frontier

IN SHIFTING OUR ATTENTION FROM the business of self-management to its roots in early childhood, it turns out that picking up our earlier discussion of marshmallows is a good place to start. Whenever I ask colleagues whether they're familiar with "the marshmallow test," invariably a handful from the leadership, innovation, and corporate worlds nod knowingly, aware of a particularly revealing marshmallow-related challenge (which I discuss in the WILL Skills chapter). Just as likely to respond yes, however, are those in the worlds of early childhood development and psychology who are familiar with another, equally revealing test sometimes referred to as Mischel's Stanford marshmallow experiment.[9] Stanford psychologist Walter Mischel began this ME-focused experiment, considered by some to be one of the best-known studies in the history of psychology, nearly forty years ago.[10]

Mischel's landmark research, relatively simple in design, sought to better understand the development of self-control and deferred gratification in early childhood and whether these abilities had any implications for future life outcomes. Preschool test subjects were, one by one, brought into a room where a single marshmallow sat before them on a table. The children were told that if they waited a full fifteen minutes for the researcher to return to the room, they would be rewarded with two marshmallows instead of just one. If they couldn't wait, they were told all they had to do was ring the bell and the researcher would promptly return, but they'd only get to eat a single marshmallow. And with that, each child was left alone to face the sweet temptation. The children's internal struggles caught on video were both adorable and revealing.

The children spanned the self-restraint spectrum. Some succumbed immediately to temptation and ate the marshmallow. Others were able to wait long enough to be rewarded with a second marshmallow. Those who managed to resist giving in to their temptation did so by exercising any number of clever techniques—some covered their eyes, turned around so they couldn't see it, tugged their hair, or even stroked the marshmallow like a tiny stuffed pet.

But that was only the beginning. Follow-up studies decades later revealed that the preschoolers who waited the longest were more likely to have better life outcomes: they were better students, had more refined social skills, earned more money, and were healthier. They were also less likely to abuse drugs, go to jail, or become obese. In short, Mischel's marshmallow work, and several subsequent studies like it, suggests that a young child's ability to demonstrate self-control has implications that extend well beyond the preschool years. Obviously, Mischel's findings and the ME Skills he studied apply to far more than just marshmallows.

More importantly, at least in my mind, Mischel discovered that the "low-delayers"—those who couldn't wait for the second marshmallow—could actually learn to become "high delayers." Furthermore, a follow-up brain imaging study forty years later revealed visible differences between the two groups in the prefrontal cortex, the part of the brain that serves as home to executive function skills.[11] That's what's so instructive about these findings: they highlight the potential opportunity we have to teach young children self-control and other ME Skills and, by doing so, help them reap significant rewards for decades to come.

The Predictive Power of Childhood Self-Control

IN 2011, THE PROCEEDINGS OF the National Academy of Sciences published an article called "A Gradient of Childhood Self-Control Predicts Health, Wealth, and Public Safety."[12] Edited by Nobel Prize–winning economist James Heckman and authored by a group of highly distinguished researchers whose fields span an array of disciplines, including psychology, neuroscience, psychiatry, and the behavioral sciences, it opened with a ME Skills–related statement that's profoundly relevant for us, as parents: "The need to delay gratification, control impulses, and modulate emotional expression is the earliest and most ubiquitous demand that societies place on their children, and success at many life tasks depends critically on children's mastery of such self-control."

In this study, researchers used a standard measure of self-control to assess more than a thousand children as young as three years old. As in Mischel's research, they followed up decades later and found that differences in self-control in early childhood predicted a whole range of future life outcomes, including physical health, drug use, personal finances, and criminal offenses over the subsequent thirty years.

Highly regarded as one of the leading researchers in the area of self-control, University of Pennsylvania psychologist Angela

Duckworth astutely captures the bearing these skills have. She likens self-regulation in preschool to resiliency and grit later in life.[13,14] The implications are clear: the extent to which young children demonstrate ME Skills matters a lot, not only when it comes to not biting marshmallows or friends but also in the long term.

The ABCs of Mindfulness

WITH ALL OF THIS TALK about self-management and self-control, it can seem like I'm suggesting that our children should robotically suppress their emotions. But, in fact, ME Skills are quite the opposite. With ME Skills, children learn to become *aware* of their emotions and how they're feeling so that they can gradually learn how to channel those thoughts and feelings more effectively and productively. In fact, it's often the children lacking self-awareness at a very young age who tend to lash out and act destructively when they feel angry, hurt, or jealous (in preschool and, later, in the workplace). When a child isn't aware of how he feels, controlling or redirecting those common emotions can be practically impossible. Self-control, self-management, and self-restraint can only happen if children learn to identify how they are feeling in the first place. This also sets the foundation for WE Skills, which involve understanding others' emotions, but children must first become aware of their own feelings before being able to take that next step.

Mindfulness is an important tool for bridging the gap between young children being aware of how they're feeling and learning how to manage their behavior. A recent study in the journal *Developmental Psychology* found that when preschoolers participated in a twelve-week-long program in which they practiced the ABCs of mindfulness—attention, breath and body, and caring—they earned higher marks in academic performance and—more pertinent to ME Skills—improved in areas of self-regulation such as emotional and impulse control.[15] As we've learned from studies discussed previously, these skills are associated with greater success later in life.

Of course we can't realistically expect two- and three-year-olds to sit and count to ten before reacting—you're lucky if you can get a toddler to sit still for ten seconds at all. However, they can learn to pause for a breath and notice their physical sensations. Parents often jump in prematurely or react in frustration when their child has a temper tantrum or struggles emotionally in other ways, when in fact encouraging and helping kids practice mindfulness makes them more capable of managing their emotions than we might realize. Many small children just require a few moments to figure out what they're feeling, how to deal with their emotional upsets, and practice self-soothing.

My daughter used to have classic two-year-old temper tantrums. Rather than trying to "fix" her feelings or send her to her room, my husband and I would ask, "Do you need to take some time away?" She would yell, "Yes!" and march up to her room. As she retreated, we would tell her that we were going to miss her and to let us know when she felt better and wanted to rejoin us. Sometimes she'd stay upstairs in her room for quite a long while, and we'd ask whether she was ready to come down. Sometimes she'd say no. But when she was ready, she'd wander back calmer and more in control of her emotions. Although this level of self-awareness isn't something we can expect from all young kids—it certainly wasn't the case with our other two children—giving children the opportunity to at least pause, take a deep breath, and regroup (mindfulness in action) for a few moments is an important way to foster ME Skills early in life.

The Developmental Milestones of ME

ELLEN GALINSKY, PRESIDENT AND COFOUNDER of the Families and Work Institute, offers up a wealth of studies involving young children that suggest their capacity for focus and self-management is much greater than many people expect. On the basis of extensive research shared in her book, Mind in the Making, Galinsky clearly identifies focus and self-control as skill number one. As she explains, "Focus and self-control begin with paying attention . . . an ability that children are born with."[16] Thus, the cumulative, research-based message is clear: we, as parents, can actually *teach* our children how to cultivate their inner focus, improve their self-awareness and self-management, and strengthen their ME Skills. Galinsky builds on this message in concluding, "These skills are like muscles—the more we work on them, the stronger they become."[17]

There's clearly a lot at stake when it comes to our children's ME Skills development, which makes our role as parents figuring out how best to understand, recognize, and cultivate them incredibly valuable. First and foremost, it's worth noting that the basic development of self-control, self-motivation, and self-awareness starts taking place before the age of five. During their first three years, infants and toddlers depend heavily on adults to help them experience, regulate, and express emotions, as well as learn what people expect of them. A child's ability to manage and express emotions really picks up pace around age three. Therefore, much of what young children do and what's expected of them as they get older is determined by the early development of ME Skills.

- **Newborn to six months:** From a very young age, babies start to become developmentally capable of a basic but essential element of self-control: self-soothing. Already able to bring their hands to their mouth and suck on them (prenatal ultrasounds sometimes even reveal babies sucking their fingers in utero), two-month-olds use this simple and often taken-for-granted strategy to calm themselves (albeit briefly) without the need for any outside intervention. Very young babies also manifest budding emotional awareness, exhibited when they display the ever-so-eagerly anticipated social smile, an expression that convincingly conveys emotional meaning. Very early on, babies also start to become more aware of and adept at sharing additional emotions more intentionally, employing crying and fussiness to let those around them know their feelings.

With respect to focus and attention, young babies can also pay attention, granted not yet as intently or for as long of periods of time as later in life. Even in the earliest weeks, babies can fix and focus on their parents' faces. By two months, they pay closer attention to faces and can "fix and follow" objects that are moved across their field of vision.

The gradual disappearance of many of the newborn reflexes (which, by definition, are involuntary, automatic responses to stimuli) over the first several months allows babies to start improving their self-control in a physical sense as well. By about four months, they demonstrate their newfound ability not only to bring their hands across their bodies in front of their faces (described as "crossing midline" in formal milestone lingo) but also, in characteristic four-month-old fashion, to stare at them in amazement. This budding self-awareness coupled with improving self-control also leads to babies using their hands and eyes together in a more coordinated fashion, resulting in fun new abilities such as seeing a toy and successfully reaching for or batting at it.

- **Six months to one year:** Nothing says budding self-awareness like a six-month-old recognizing himself in the mirror or responding to his name. Emotions at this age also become easier for us to recognize, as six-month-olds characteristically start making sounds that more specifically (and understandably) convey their joy and displeasure.

- **One to two years:** Twelve-month-olds start to play favorites whether in the form of toys, books, or parents. This soon leads to the appearance of the temper tantrums characteristic of eighteen-month-olds, who have a much clearer sense of self, emotions, and wants but who aren't yet capable of self-management (more commonly identified in the parenting world as impulse control—or the lack thereof). Self-management is a skill, you'll recall, that depends on the prefrontal cortex and executive function skills that don't really pick up in their development until around the age of three.

  As children celebrate their first birthdays, they continue to increasingly interact with people and the environment around them and are able to focus for longer periods of time than they could as infants—long enough to follow the path of an object as it falls, for example. This example also illustrates the developing ability to concentrate on objects or people even when they are out of sight, an attention skill first demonstrated by nine-month-olds' characteristic (not to mention endearing) interest in playing peek-a-boo.

  In terms of physical self-control, the second year is full of "do-it-myself" firsts, from walking and exploring independently to drinking from a cup and eating with a spoon by the middle of the year. Children round out their second year with increasing independence that can show itself in the form of defiant behavior (i.e., doing what they are told not to).

- **Three years:** Typically by age three, children start using the words "I," "me" and "mine" and grasping their implications. Similarly, the ability to focus and pay attention has developed to the point that they can follow two- or three-step instructions. Their emerging self-control enables three-year-olds to sit still occasionally and to concentrate more on activities like copying a circle or building simple three- or four-piece puzzles.

- **Four years:** And, finally, although four-year-olds typically become less me-centric, as evidenced by their newfound preference for playing and cooperating with other children over playing by themselves, they still may talk predominantly (and sometimes incessantly) about themselves and their interests as well as play by themselves.

Cookie Monster, Preschoolers, and Self-Control

LET'S RETURN FOR A MOMENT to Mischel's marshmallow experiment, considered a landmark in highlighting the importance of developing early ME Skills for future success. Mischel's influence has extended far beyond his Stanford psychology lab—all the way to Sesame Street, in fact. According to Sesame Workshop's senior vice president of Curriculum and Content Dr. Rosemarie Truglio,[18] she and her team of early childhood experts recognized the need to focus more attention on better helping their preschool audience learn the executive function and self-regulatory skills that Mischel's marshmallows originally brought to light. Whereas Cookie Monster seemed to be perfectly suited for this all-important role, the team knew that learning to resist temptations would be hard work, for young kids and endearing blue cookie monsters alike. Recognizing that there was not going to be a simple one-size-fits-all strategy that would work for all children, and committed to getting it right, they consulted none other than Walter Mischel himself, who helped review their approach, which included a particular ME Skill–focused episode called "Get Lost, Mr. Chips," developed specifically to teach preschoolers about self-control and some basic ways to master it.[19]

In this September 24, 2012, episode, Cookie Monster wishes to become a member of the Cookie Connoisseurs Club, the most exclusive cookie appreciation club in the country. Membership requires him to follow the three rules of cookie tasting—looking at, smelling, and nibbling—all of which means he has to do a significantly better job of resisting his cookie-devouring impulses. Cookie Monster believes he can follow these rules but ends up devouring the first cookie right away. Given another chance, he tries to distract himself by pretending that the cookie is an inedible object (a yo-yo). Once he smells the cookie, however, he eats it right up, an impulse that repeats itself even when he tries to pretend that the cookie smells bad by smelling a stinky boot. With each failed attempt, the show successfully conveys the message that learning to resist temptation can be tough and takes practice. Given an additional chance to prove himself, Cookie Monster employs yet another self-regulatory strategy known as "self-talk" that involves reminding himself out loud of what's at stake and that he needs to control himself so he can stay in the club. This strategy works!

What caught my attention—beyond the fact that the importance of teaching young children ME Skills had successfully made its way all the way to Sesame Street—was what happened when researcher Deborah Linebarger at the University of Iowa Children's Media Lab subsequently studied the impact of such executive function curriculum-driven show segments.[20] When put through the equivalent of the Stanford marshmallow experiment (i.e., wait longer, get a bigger reward), preschoolers who had viewed video clips of Cookie Monster practicing self-control were able to wait more than four minutes longer, on average, than those who had viewed unrelated content. This tells us two things: that young children are receptive to and benefit greatly from being taught ME Skills behaviors and strategies, and that intentional, wide-scale efforts, like having Cookie Monster demonstrate self-regulatory strategies to his millions of preschool followers, have the potential to successfully help them "develop stronger executive function skills that will positively impact them in the short term across social/emotional and cognitive domains as well as contribute substantially to both later school and life success."[21]

In addition to recognizing the significance of promoting ME Skills directly to preschoolers, it was not lost on Sesame Street's social media team that making the importance of ME Skills clear to parents and caregivers of young children was similarly worthwhile.[22] Sesame Street thus created an entertaining song called "Me Want It (But Me Wait)," complete with its own hashtag, #controlmeself.[23] In the song, Cookie Monster amusingly demonstrates just what it takes to master self-control when faced with temptation. The catchy, rhyming song includes clever lyrics such as follows:

> When me lose control, when me on the brink
> Need to just calm down, me need to stop and think.
> Me need control me self, yeah that's the way to live!
> And then me functioning like an executive!

And:

> When me lose control, when me have no doubt
> Me have strategies that can calm me down.
> Me can talk to self. Me can stand up straight.
> Me can take deep breath. Me can self-regulate!

What You Can Do to Help ME

WHILE COMPELLING EVIDENCE POINTS TO the potential of using media to help our children learn, we still know that nothing more positively affects young children and their ability to learn than direct, social interactions with us, their parents. With this in mind, below are some ways you can model ME Skills for your children and other activities you can use to help them learn self-management, mindfulness, and more.

Remember that building ME Skills—and all QI Skills, for that matter—is a gradual process, and it's important to maintain realistic expectations based on where your child is developmentally. So, instead of getting angry when you notice a distinct lack of ME Skills (like the classic two-year-old meltdown in the candy aisle at Target), try seeing it as an opportunity to help your child learn how to practice better self-control in that moment.

Be a super model. Infants, toddlers, and preschoolers alike learn by observing the people around them, even more than we realize. Researchers at Indiana University recently conducted what could be considered a put-your-cell-phone-down-and-pay-attention-to-your-baby study. In considering the impact of social interaction on an infant's attention, they found a direct connection between how long a parent looked at an object and how long that parent's infant remained focused on the same object.[24] In other words, from day one we have plenty of great, everyday opportunities to show our children what attention and focus look like. Whether you play with your baby or let your preschooler watch you spend an hour working intently on a home improvement project or concentrate your energies on a complicated jigsaw puzzle, your demonstration of applied focus and attention will pay significant ME Skill dividends, especially when you do so without picking up your cell phone or becoming distracted in other ways.

Rely on routines. Routines provide children with security, predictability, and comfort. This makes routines a wonderful opportunity for fostering ME Skills. That's because routines give children a system in which to operate, knowing what's expected of them and gradually learning to control themselves within it. For example, as early as you can, establish a simple yet solid bedtime routine for your children, which can involve giving them a bath, brushing their teeth, helping them put on their pajamas, reading them a book, and then putting them to bed. With consistency and practice (and some setbacks and testing of limits, of course, as well as successes), over time kids become skilled at controlling their impulses when they have a process they can rely on.

Enhance emotional vocabulary. Managing one's own emotions is a cornerstone of ME Skills. A child needs to first understand how she's feeling before she can learn to control her own reactions and behaviors. Whereas many children learn "happy" and "mad" early on, it's up to us to help them learn to name all of the subtle feelings in between that can more accurately describe how they're feeling in any particular instance. This can go a long way in also helping to prevent tantrums, since it's often when kids feel like they don't have the tools to appropriately express themselves that they are most likely to get frustrated and lash out. Here are some simple and fun ways that you can help expand your child's emotional vocabulary:

- Use a wider range of feeling words in your own vocabulary when you talk to your toddler. Consider introducing words such as *surprised, frustrated, overwhelmed, confused, relaxed, relieved, proud, brave, concerned*, and more.
- Draw or look at pictures of faces and help your child describe how that face is feeling.
- Read lots of children's books. Discuss with your child how he thinks different characters are feeling in the pictures and in the storylines, and ask him how he would feel in similar situations.

Encourage emotional expression. All it may take is asking, "How are you feeling?" Try to get your child to articulate in her own words what's going on inside. Be careful not to criticize her expression of feelings or explain why she shouldn't feel the way she does. This is trickier to do than it may seem. As parents, we may try to explain why our child shouldn't feel a certain way when we want her to feel better about something, but we run the risk of discouraging emotional expression when we downplay her emotions. Instead, try saying, "I'm very sorry you feel that way," or "You seem upset. Can you tell me why?" You don't have to agree with her reasoning for being upset, for example, but you can still acknowledge and even sympathize with her emotion as you help teach her what a more acceptable way of handling it would be.

Use "time away" instead of "time-out." When a young child resorts to screaming, kicking, biting, or otherwise "losing control," your instinct may be to put him in "time-out" to teach him that those behaviors aren't acceptable. Although his inciting behaviors may well be clearly unacceptable, the problem with time-outs is that they all too often are overshadowed by a significant degree of parental frustration and anger—two emotions that unfortunately do very little, if anything, to create a positive learning experience. That's why I suggest affording children "time away" instead. Now, I am well aware that many of you will be wondering what, exactly, is the difference? Let me assure you that the distinction, though subtle, is not purely semantic. Rather, the difference between time-out and time away involves a fundamental change in parental mindset. Yes, "time away" still inherently involves physically removing children from environments or situations in which they become overwhelmed or act out. But rather than as a form of punishment, time away should be seen and treated as a way to give young children the space and time they need to get themselves, their emotions, and their behaviors under control. Of course, this won't be an instantaneous process. But instead of yelling and getting angry (which do little to support the mastery of challenging new social and behavioral skills), commit to controlling your own emotions while you firmly but calmly guide your child away from inciting situations so he can get himself and his behavior managed.

Take turns. Playing games that require turn taking inherently encourages young children to exercise self-control and impulse control while practicing focus and attention because they have to wait until it's their chance to go. Peek-a-boo is one of the earliest games babies pick up that involves not only focus and attention but also taking turns. As your child gets a bit older, try alternating stacking blocks, narrating this turn-taking activity as you go by saying, "Now it's your turn," and "Now it's my turn." With pre-schoolers, playing stop-and-go games such as Simon Says; Duck, Duck, Goose; Red Light, Green Light; Mother May I; Tag; and others teaches them the value of paying close attention and patiently waiting for their turn, too.

Help your preschooler play a role. Playing, in general, hopefully conjures up happy childhood memories and makes you think of imagination and creativity (skills we focus on more closely in the WHAT IF chapter); it also has the potential to provide ME benefits as well. By encouraging your preschooler to engage in a more "mature" form of make-believe play that, by definition, involves taking on the role of someone else (the mommy, the daddy, a doctor, or an astronaut, for example), all sorts of additional ME Skills can be put into play. These include learning how to better restrain themselves, resist their impulses, and practice following rules. By helping your child choose a role, create an imaginary scenario, and devise related props to enter this make-believe world of role playing, you can actually facilitate better focus and attention and pave the way for them to creatively role-play for longer periods of time. [25,26]

Beware of background TV. Many of us may have the habit of leaving our televisions on even when we're not really watching, simply considering it to be harmless "background noise." Yet research shows that doing so when young children are present, even when they look directly at the TV as little as 5 percent of the time, actually negatively affects ME Skills by influencing their ability to focus and pay attention and decreasing the overall amount of time they spend playing.

Beware the Disturbing Effects of Background Television

Young children placed in a room where the TV was on in the background and tuned to a program chosen specifically for its distinct lack of kid appeal (i.e., *Jeopardy*) were nevertheless found to be less focused on their play and played for about half as long.[27]

Take a deep breath. From a very young age, we teach kids how to point, wave, walk, and talk, but we often forget to teach them one of the most basic, yet important skills of all: how to breathe. Sure, breathing may come naturally, but learning how to control their own breath turns out to also be an effective tool for exercising mindfulness, focusing attention, and managing emotions. Professor Richard Davidson and his team at the University of Wisconsin's Center for Healthy Minds have done just that in developing techniques for helping preschool teachers instill this valuable skill.[28] This can be as simple as having children lie on their backs, placing a small (but not choking-hazard small) object on their stomachs, and then having them watch it rise and fall with each breath. With regular practice, young children can master the skill, even in the absence of an object, and can then be encouraged to take bigger and deeper breaths to help calm their minds and bodies whenever their emotions start to spiral out of control.

Rest and recess. Whether you're two, four, or twenty-four, self-management skills are at their best when you're well rested and have had a chance to move your body. If you find your child is having regular tantrums or struggling with self-control in other ways (hitting, biting, or kicking others, for example), consider how she's been napping lately, how she's sleeping at night, and whether she's getting enough physical activity during the day. Remember, putting ME Skills into practice is a learning process, and it is well recognized that physical activity and being well rested can go a long way toward helping kids be in good shape to better exercise their self-control abilities. It has been shown that executive functions suffer first and most when children do not get enough sleep, making it harder for them to think clearly or exercise good self-control.[29]

5

QI Skill 2

WE

Learning to Play Well with Others

Alone we can do so little; together we can do
so much.

—Helen Keller

The biggest deficit that we have in our society
and the world right now is an empathy deficit. We
are in great need of people being able to stand
in somebody else's shoes and see the world
through their eyes.

—President Barack Obama, "Empathy
Documentary—Barack Obama Promotes
Empathy from Books and Literacy,"
YouTube video

STARTING IN THE 1950S, ESTHER Lederer and Pauline Phillips dedicated themselves to helping solve people's social
and relationship challenges. As the identical twin authors behind
"Ask Ann Landers" and "Dear Abby," respectively, their focus on

relationship skills became so popular that toward the end of the century "Dear Abby" was recognized as the world's most widely syndicated column, appearing in twelve hundred newspapers, translated into more than twenty languages, and boasting an audience of ninety million readers.[1]

The second half of the twentieth century also bore witness to the meteoric rise of Oprah Winfrey. Credited by *Time* magazine for her fundamental shift from "report talk" (the formal, Phil Donohue-esque reporting of the news that had prevailed for decades) to a more "intimate" form of "*rapport* talk,"[2] Oprah created the highest-rated program of its kind in history by connecting with her expansive audience on a much more personal level. The fact that she was deemed the most influential woman in the world says a lot—not only about Oprah but about the value our culture places on the more social aspects of life, from relationships and personal connectedness, to listening, social skills, and empathy.[3]

Clearly, assigning value to social skills and relationships isn't something altogether new. It's just that in the twentieth century these were largely relegated to print and television, as people were strongly encouraged to check their emotions at the office door lest they cloud thinking and impair productivity. Thus, we went about our business at work, and then went home to fill our need for social connectedness. Today social-emotional skills are front and center, and their domain has expanded considerably to include today's business world, where communication, collaboration, empathy, and teamwork reign supreme. In other words, the very thing that drove the success of the syndicated columns and talk shows of the last century has crossed far into the twenty-first-century world of business. What, exactly, is that "thing"? It's the power of WE.

What Are WE Skills?

IN THE MOST INTUITIVE SENSE of the term, WE Skills are *people* skills. They're all about forming relationships and interacting with others. When you think of WE-skilled adults, you think of those who communicate superbly, listen attentively, and build strong, diverse relationships. WE Skills are most notably represented by today's highly coveted abilities to communicate, collaborate, and empathize with others. But they also encompass connectedness, teamwork, relationships, perspective taking, and the ability to read people. Strong WE Skills are what ultimately make it possible for us to listen to, better understand, communicate with, relate well to, and consider others' points of view.

Of all of the QI Skills, I tend to think that WE Skills' early childhood connections are the most self-explanatory. It's nearly impossible not to think of the world of preschool when discussing what's at the heart of WE Skills. After all, it only takes a quick translation to come up with the preschool equivalents of "put your listening ears on," "use your words," "think about how you'd feel," and "learn to share and play nice with others in the same sandbox." These are phrases that anyone in the business of raising and teaching two-, three-, and four-year-olds routinely employ. They also represent the early assembly of some of the most valuable skills in a child's developing QI Skill toolkit.

The fact is that we've always been interested in helping our children learn to play well with others. We teach them to use their words (instead of their hands or teeth) when they want something, use their manners (instead of whining or shouting), and share (instead of hoarding or grabbing other people's belongings). We've always done this because we care about raising our children to grow into kind, caring individuals. Whether we have been explicitly aware of it or not, parents who prioritize these behaviors have been committed to building WE Skills all along. The implications just happen to be even greater than most people realize. It's more than raising "nice" kids, which is undoubtedly an important goal. Strong WE Skills are also key to our children's future career and life success.

Relationships Matter

TODAY'S BUSINESS WORLD IS INTENSE. It's a fast-paced, globally connected, competitive arena. Yet one could also say that the business world has gone "soft"—at least with regard to its newfound emphasis on interpersonal skills. Today, everywhere you look, headlines suggest that a major shift is happening. Take, for example, a column that ran on the front page of my local newspaper's business section the morning I sat down to write this chapter. The title alone speaks volumes: "Looking for 'People' People: Solid Social Skills Top Trait Employers Seek."[4] The article shared a finding from a recent survey by the National Association of Colleges and Employers, which listed the ability to work in a team as the most desired quality they seek when hiring new graduates. Similarly, a review from the US Department of Labor reinforces the fact that a growing number of jobs in recent decades have required strong social skills.

It's not at all surprising that this shift has occurred when you consider what's happening in the world around us. Whereas individuals once worked at businesses within their own communities and climbed their way up the corporate ladder over the course of their career, today that's no longer the rule. Complex global challenges exceed the abilities of any one individual to overcome and demand collaborative efforts. Global connectedness requires people who can relate to, understand, and communicate effectively with others from different backgrounds, cultures, and belief systems even if they never actually meet on the same side of a screen. Or, as author and philosopher Suzy Kassem puts it, "To become a true global citizen, one must abandon all notions of 'otherness' and instead embrace 'togetherness.'"[5]

And if you wonder just how important sharing and togetherness are proving to be in defining today's world, consider that our new economy is now commonly referred to as the sharing economy. Whereas the twentieth century was built on hard work and rugged individualism, key competencies in the twenty-first-century workplace now include the ability to network, form alliances, and excel in a team-based atmosphere. In an era when understanding and relating to the end user are essential for a job well done, even computer programmers are no longer characterized by images of individuals sitting alone in a room. No matter the industry, everyone in business today requires the WE Skills necessary to be more productive, effective, innovative, and successful than if they attempted to go it alone.

To understand how much value is now being placed on connectedness, one needs to look no further than LinkedIn. By the end of 2015, its vast social network—designed to help individuals build their professional networks—totaled nearly four hundred million profiles worldwide and counting. Reid Hoffman, the company's cofounder, undoubtedly understands a thing or two about connectedness and the fact that relationships matter. In his book *The Start-Up of You*, Hoffman makes a profound point about the intersection of ME Skills and WE Skills, especially when it comes to working together as a team. He writes, "Your career success depends on both your individual capabilities and your network's ability to magnify them. Think of it as I^{We}. An individual's power is raised exponentially with the help of a team (a network)."[6]

I Before WE

AT A FUNDAMENTAL LEVEL, WE Skills are a natural extension of ME Skills. ME Skills are self-focused, involving both awareness and control of one's own behaviors, thoughts, and emotions; WE Skills are the outward-facing equivalent. WE Skills involve the tools necessary to understand how and why other people think, feel, and act the way they do. It's intuitive that you need to gain crucial ME Skills, such as the ability to recognize, understand, and control your own emotions, not to mention focus on and pay attention to others, before becoming skilled at relating to others (WE Skills).

If this discussion—first of ME and now of WE—is starting to remind you of the term "emotional intelligence," there's very good reason. It is, in fact, the powerful combination of ME (or, as Hoffman describes it, "I") and WE that captures the essence of emotional intelligence (often referred to as EI for short). As you may recall, this concept of EI rose to prominence in the 1990s in large part thanks to its championing by former New York Times brain and behavioral sciences reporter Daniel Goleman.[7] From his 1995 best-selling book Emotional Intelligence to his ongoing EI work as an internationally known psychologist and codirector of Rutgers's Consortium for Research on Emotional Intelligence in Organizations, Goleman has greatly contributed to solidifying the world's interest in and understanding of EI as the combination of being aware of and able to regulate one's own emotions (the very definition of our ME Skills) and the ability to empathize and build relationships with others (the foundations of WE Skills).[8]

Goldfish Crackers, Broccoli, and Toddler Altruism

In a simple yet poignant study, toddlers were shown two bowls of food, one containing goldfish crackers (chosen because of their near-universal toddler appeal), and the other, some notably less toddler-tempting broccoli. Before handing over the bowls, an experimenter ate from each and proceeded to act as if she either loved the crackers and was disgusted by the broccoli (a response meant to reflect the toddlers' own likely preferences), or just the opposite. The toddlers were then given access to the bowls. Upon being asked by the experimenter, "Could I have some?" the fourteen-month-old participants shared with the experimenter some beloved goldfish crackers regardless of how the experimenter had reacted to them.

For the eighteen-month-olds, however, the result was different. In what turned out to be a clear-cut show of understanding that someone else might actually want something different from what the toddlers wanted themselves, these slightly older children responded to the experimenter's question by handing over whichever food the *experimenter* had liked. As the researchers concluded, this shows that at as young as eighteen months—and one goldfish cracker or stalk of broccoli at a time—the basic impulses of young children can guide them beyond empathy to sharing and genuine altruism.[9]

Beyond Business

FOR THE PURPOSES OF THIS book, I'm primarily focusing on one realm (business), but it's well worth pointing out that QI Skills don't solely apply to entrepreneurs, innovators, and business leaders. Their importance is being recognized and emphasized across just about all professions, including the medical field in which I trained.

The health sector is currently number one when it comes to job growth, and it is estimated to grow even faster in the decades to come. Just as it's true for the business world, relationships matter, arguably even more so in the medical arena where everything we do is within the context of our patients. Yet health care today faces the same challenges as other professions and businesses when it comes to prioritizing people skills over the requisite technical skills. Being able to read and relate to people applies particularly well in the medical field, where we need to pick up on subtle cues that can lead us to ask more questions and gain a better understanding of our patients and their conditions. WE Skills are so crucial, in fact, that research increasingly suggests that patient outcomes, including the length of hospital stays, complication rates, and recovery times, may depend at least as much on the connections and relationships patients have with their physicians and other care providers as the medical treatments they receive.

At the same time, our next generation of health professionals continues to be at risk of entering the workforce without adequate mastery of these skills. A 2015 article in Forbes, "What Doctors Aren't Learning in Medical School and Why It Matters," specifically touches on the relevance of WE Skills in the medical field.[10] The article includes results from a survey of medical students. Ninety-six percent of them believed that effective collaboration was necessary to deliver high-quality medical care, and nearly 60 percent considered lack of communication the biggest obstacle to effective care coordination. The author of the article concludes, "Yes—they learn microbiology, biochemistry, cardiology, and orthopedics, but they [aren't learning] how to effectively and empathetically communicate, be an individual in an organization, be a leader (or a follower, for that matter), make patients happy, run an effective meeting, [and] market themselves or their practice."

Just as WE Skills are woven into the fabric of twenty-first-century business environments, the world in general is searching for people equipped with an impressive set of WE Skills. We can see the need for improved development in nearly all industries, including health care.

Leading the Way with WE

IN PLACING INCREASED VALUE ON WE Skills, forward-thinking organizations are transforming how they function at every level. As organizations continue to flatten and move from pyramid to team structures, they increasingly depend on strong collaborations that break down the walls that once divided cubicles from corner offices. More than ever before, companies are hiring and rewarding people who "play well" with others.

Today, WE Skills provide a new lens through which companies routinely look as they hire, promote, and develop their employees. As an extension of that, organizations are also looking to a different style of leadership than in the past. Instead of seeking the prototypical boss—decisive, authoritarian, and just plain bossy—they seek out people with contemporary leadership qualities, which now include empathy, flexibility, and relationship-building skills.

Key among those skills is a person's ability to stand up and take the lead when necessary, but also to know when it's more effective to step back and allow someone else on the team to take the reins. Given the complexity of juggling people's talents and egos, this represents no easy task. However, I can't help but think about how this ability is not just innate but also one that can be learned very early.

Consider the game of Duck, Duck, Goose. This nearly universal preschool game requires individuals to step (or run) forward when it's their turn but also to calmly sit back down, listen, and pay attention when it's not. These happen to be essential qualities in a twenty-first-century leader. Although I'm not suggesting that a friendly round or two of Duck, Duck, Goose becomes a required team-building activity in the workplace (it probably wouldn't hurt), I am suggesting that the WE Skills our children learn and develop in the course of their everyday play have big-picture relevance that extends well beyond the preschool playground.

WE in Early Childhood

THOUGH SIMILAR IN CONCEPT, WE Skills start out looking a bit different in preschools and playrooms than those you'll ultimately encounter in offices and boardrooms. Communication, collaboration, and teamwork define WE Skills in adulthood; young children, however, have a long way to go before they master those abilities. Instead, in the early years WE Skills can be broken down into their foundational forms of language, listening, and understanding others' emotions. These are, after all, the skills that enable young children to learn to play nice, communicate, share, and make friends.

Nothing makes the case for how much these early WE Skills stand to influence your child's future success better than a study you may recall from the chapter WHY EARLY. In research led by my Penn State colleague Mark Greenberg, one of the top social-emotional researchers in the country, kindergarten teachers were asked to rate their students' social and communication skills, assigning points based on qualities such as "cooperates with peers," "shares materials," "is helpful to others," "is very good at understanding feelings," and "resolves problems on their own." When researchers checked in on how the five-year-old test subjects were faring up to nineteen years later, they found that for every one point increase in the original scores, the children were 54 percent more likely to have earned a high school diploma, twice as likely to have attained a college degree in early adulthood, and nearly 50 percent more likely to have a full-time job at age twenty-five.[11]

As even earlier core aspects of WE Skills, language and listening skills also play a foundational and predictive role. Now, at first glance, these skills may seem a bit like ME Skills because they're more individually based. But though it is true that hearing is a relatively internal, cognitive process that involves the brain receiving and processing sound, effective *listening*, on the other hand, is clearly a relationship-based WE Skill that is key to effective communication. Just think of the phrase, "I know you can hear me, but are you *listening* to me?" Listening is the social application of hearing, and thus represents a two-way street that requires us to hear the words and, more importantly, to comprehend the emotions, message, and intent behind what's said. Similarly, when it comes to language, the ability to speak and "use your words" is what provides children the strong foundation on which to build their ability to communicate, share ideas, and connect with others.

> "Every human being needs to listen consciously in order to live fully—connected in space and in time to the physical world around us, connected in understanding to each other."
>
> —*Sound Business* author Julian Treasure, in "Five Ways to Listen Better," TEDGlobal, 2011

Getting Acquainted with WE Milestones

IT'S EASY TO SEE WE Skills taking root very early when you know what to look for. We know that babies are born with a drive to relate to, connect with, and learn from others. As you'll recall from WHY EARLY, some of the most revealing modern baby brain research examines the earliest forms of foundational learning, language, and communication. The development of these skills is astoundingly socially dependent. Social interactions with caring, responsive adults (parents, most often) trigger babies' brains to become sponges for knowledge. This means that as we go about responding to and interacting with our babies day to day, we're not only teaching them social skills but helping to shape their brains in ways that enable them to develop even stronger WE Skills in the future.

Social interactions are the basis upon which baby brains develop, and are therefore well reflected in the milestones babies reach. Here are some key WE milestones you can watch for and help your child master throughout the first five years:

- **Two months:** By two months old, babies master the social smile they've been practicing since birth, making it much easier to distinguish it from gas or a reflex. As an early indication that they're listening to what's going on in the world around them, they now turn their heads attentively toward sounds.

- **Four months:** Babies at this age routinely smile at people spontaneously, enjoy playing with others, and respond to any affection that comes their way with smiles and coos. They copy other people's expressions and sounds and, in applying what they've heard, soon begin to babble.

- **Six months:** As signs of their budding language development, six-month-olds make new and increasingly meaningful sounds, such as stringing vowels together while babbling ("ah," "eh," "oh"). They also become better two-way communicators as they more purposefully use gestures that include facial expressions, actions, and sounds to respond to others. In a show of budding social competence and emotional maturation, typical six-month-olds like to play with others, especially their parents, respond to other people's emotions, and engage in "conversations" by making sounds in response to those they hear from other people.

- **Nine months:** In a fun display of increasing social interaction and intentional vocalization, nine-month-olds are known for their endearing ability to make recognizable sounds, including "mama," "dada," and "baba." Developing social awareness includes being able to identify (and respond differently) to familiar versus unfamiliar people—a social "skill" that may cause them to develop a bit of stranger anxiety or become clingy with the people with whom they feel the most comfortable. Nine-month-olds also develop a skill called "shared attention" (also referred to as "joint attention" or "gaze shifting") that allows them to share a common focus on something such as a person or object in their surroundings. In other words, you look at a book, your baby follows your gaze and, as a result, focuses his or her attention on the same book. This ability represents a fundamentally social one, as it is akin to "being on the same wavelength" or "sharing a thought" with another person. It also happens to be a skill now considered to be at the heart of language development because it allows nine-month-olds to understand what you're directing their attention to as you point to things and name them.

Do You See What I See?

The seemingly simple but fundamentally social ability of older infants (ten- and eleven-month-olds) to follow the gaze of an adult to see what they are looking at—often referred to as *joint* or *shared attention*—has been positively correlated with subsequent measures of their language abilities as toddlers (at eighteen months of age).[12]

- **Twelve months:** As children enter toddlerhood, they are now able to recognize meaningful words, respond to simple requests, use simple gestures like shaking their head no or waving bye-bye, and make sounds with changes in tone (similar to adult speech). They also begin showing more concern for others. Even though children as young as twelve months may well demonstrate early acts of empathy—sometimes in the form of a hug, pat, or touch—this doesn't guarantee that they'll do so all the time, or as often as you might like.

- **Eighteen months:** Language and communication skills continue to grow. Your child may say several single words, shake his head "no," and point to show you what he wants. At this stage, he may show increasing interest in other people's wants, needs, and feelings in such endearing ways as pretending to feed a doll or stuffed animal, handing things to others while playing, showing affection to familiar people, asking "are you okay?" and sharing or offering things such as bandages or a blanket to try to make others feel better.

- **Two years:** On the language front, children can now name familiar people (as well as body parts), identify objects in books, put together two- to four-word sentences, follow simple instructions, and actively repeat words overheard in conversations. Whereas prior to age two, children tend to engage in "parallel" play in which they may be in the same space as other kids but play by themselves in their own universe, around the age of two they start to get more excited about engaging other children in their play. This represents a significantly more social shift in the way they interact and play. Between ages two and three, children usually know just how it feels to be happy, sad, and angry; know the names for these emotions; and, just as importantly, can usually relate to others' feelings of happiness, sadness, and anger as well. When children this age are confronted by more complicated feelings that they can't yet label, though, such as frustration or embarrassment, don't be surprised if their ability to communicate or empathize falters.

- **Three years:** In preschoolers, WE Skills really start to blossom. This makes sense from a developmental standpoint since children start to practice applying their much more rapidly developing social abilities as they learn to take turns, compromise, contemplate how others might feel, and share. In addition to mastering words and concepts like "I," "me," "we," and "you" and understanding the idea of "mine" and "his" or "hers," they show affection for friends without prompting. They also become more adept at social play and often like to play with dolls, animals, and people as they go about their very important business of acting out and practicing social interactions.

- **Four years:** At four, children gain a better grasp of language and communication with the ability to tell stories, sing songs from memory (get ready for many renditions of "Wheels on the Bus"), and correctly use pronouns such as "he" and "she." Pre-kindergarteners also become more adept at perspective taking with make-believe play games and dress-up as they pretend to be "Mom," "Dad," and other familiar figures in their lives. Interactive games tend to be especially appealing to most four-year-olds, who would rather play with others than by themselves. The success of these increasingly social activities is, by the way, greatly enhanced as the ability to cooperate sets in.

Encouraging WE Skills in a Wee World

THE MOST IMPORTANT THING YOU can do to help foster your child's WE Skills is to provide plenty of opportunities for your child to witness WE Skills in action and practice them. Remember that, like learning to read, learning how to read other people is a complicated process that takes lots of time, practice, mistakes, and the opportunity to learn from those mistakes. Young children are in the process of learning how emotions work and how people get along with each other. So, although it's important to encourage children to practice their WE Skills, it's equally important not to expect perfection. You can help your child develop WE Skills through modeling the behaviors you want to see, talking them through it when they make mistakes, and creating valuable learning experiences that can include play dates and preschool. Here are a few more specific ways you can help your child make the leap from ME to WE.

"Emotional literacy is not just a gift; it's actually an ability that can be taught to our children, starting when they are young as toddlers . . . though the seeds are planted even earlier, by how we relate and respond to our infants."

—Michele Borba, *UnSelfie: Why Empathetic Kids Succeed in Our All-About-Me World*

Help them put their listening ears on. We know that the better children become at listening, the better able they are at both learning and interacting with others. Start by modeling attentive listening, since offering your focused attention and responding to your baby's cries, coos, and conversations can go a long way toward influencing your child in how to do the same. As your child's turn-taking abilities develop, make it a habit to reinforce that active listening inherently involves not interrupting (an ability that requires impulse control ME Skills and that is admittedly easier to discuss than it is for a preschooler to master!). Consider borrowing from the *Tools of the Mind* playbook by making and having your child use note cards—one with a pair of lips and the other with an ear—as tangible reminders of when she's supposed to speak and when she's supposed to listen.[13] Because part of what makes a good listener is the ability to set aside distractions, also make a point of minimizing your multitasking and committing time to really stop and listen to your child. Take advantage of the sounds of the world around you to encourage your child to be more aware. This can be as easy as taking a walk outside and playing "what's that sound?" by directing your child's attention to the rustle of leaves in the wind, the sound of water flowing in a river, or any of the other "noises" in nature that become noticeable when you more actively listen for them.

Encourage active listening. Active listening, by definition, requires concentration (a ME Skill) combined with an understanding of what someone else is saying. Fortunately, reading aloud with your child happens to be one of the very best ways to encourage and develop this all-important skill. Remember that the value of listening isn't just about hearing the words but more importantly about understanding their message. Be sure to encourage your toddler to comment on and ask and answer questions about each story rather than just passively listening. Also be aware that active listening does not necessarily require children to sit perfectly still (a concept we will discuss further in the WIGGLE Skills chapter).

Use your words. By simply using *your* words, you can encourage toddlers to use theirs. As their vocabularies grow, providing young children with the words and opportunities to use them is especially important for the constructive communication aspect of WE Skills development. When you find that your toddler is struggling to communicate ideas, wants, needs, frustrations, or emotions, help him along by commenting on or putting into words what you think he is feeling and asking him clarifying questions such as, "Are you upset because you wanted to read another book?" In early childhood, as in life, learning to use one's words helps improve one's ability to play well with others, if for no other reason than because the inability to do so often results in less socially tolerated behaviors such as hitting, biting, and throwing objects or tantrums, to name but a few.

Teach them to "play nice." Create ample opportunities for your child to put her budding listening, language, sharing, turn-taking, and empathy skills into practice by being around other children.

It has long been said that play is the "work" of three-year-olds, whether it takes place in the form of play dates, preschool, or play-time at the park. This is true for many reasons, not the least of which is the fact that this is the age when children begin making leaps and bounds in their understanding of, showing affection for, and interacting with other children. That's not to say that the shift from individual (or parallel) play characteristic of one- and two-year-olds to the more interactive, social play of three-year-olds happens smoothly and overnight. Rather, it takes plenty of playtime and practice to learn to play nice.

Let them walk in someone else's shoes. Giving young children opportunities to dress up and role-play, both popular pastimes of preschoolers, allows them the chance to literally and figuratively put themselves in others' shoes. When they pretend to be some-one else, they're practicing perspective taking. They're starting to understand where someone else is coming from because they have to imagine what it would be like to think, feel, and act like some-one else. A few dress-up supplies can go a long way toward getting the ball rolling helping them imagine creative scenarios—whether that's playing school, doctor, or house—and strengthening the early roots of perspective taking.

Demonstrate reading and responding to body language. Because your child first learns how to respond to others by watching you, make a point very early on to carefully observe and respond to your baby's physical movements and other nonverbal cues. As soon as you start to look for them, you're sure to discover that even infants use natural signals to communicate. Infants who smack their lips may be hungry, while those who turn their heads away probably are not. Toddlers who cover their face or turn their back are usu-ally trying to tell you something. Attentive caregivers who notice and respond to young children's hand and body movements help pave the way for children to become aware of and able to interpret other people's emotions, intentions, and perspective, even in the absence of words.

Try out baby signs. Months before young children can actually speak, they are able to master the motor skills necessary for what can be described as "manual modes" of communication, including meaningful gesturing such as waving and pointing and the more formal movements that constitute sign language. Typical twelve- to eighteen-month-olds' spoken vocabulary is limited to a handful of words. Yet babies as young as six to nine months possess the motor skills to start learning how to sign and are soon able to communicate an impressively wide range of practical concepts such as *eat, sleep, more, milk, book, diaper, please, thank you, mom, dad,* and *all done*. This makes baby sign language a particularly fun and interactive way to help get your baby's WE Skills development off to a great start. What's more, it is now believed that teaching babies sign language may actually help, rather than interfere with, the development of verbal language. If the idea of learning sign language seems a bit daunting, rest assured there are plenty of books and apps that can help you learn the basics quickly and easily.

Make helping others a routine. At the heart of getting along well with people is being kind and caring about them. Even very young toddlers come by this skill naturally, offering a hug or showing concern for others. So, one of your most important roles, other than just modeling kind and caring behavior yourself, is to make sure young children have daily opportunities to practice thinking about and doing things for someone else. Early on, this can be as simple as praising a toddler who shows sympathy or concern for someone who is upset or recognizing a preschooler who shares a toy with a friend or sibling. As your child gets a bit older, make it a point to regularly reach out as a family to help each other and others and contribute to causes that your child can relate to (such as food donation, supporting a local homeless or pet shelter, coat or mitten donations). These are great ways to let kids feel like active participants.

Ask, "How would you feel?" Asking your child to think about how they'd feel is a fundamentally important question to ask early and often. This is especially true in instances where your child may have done something not so nice to another child (such as hitting or snatching a toy). Helping your child think about the golden rule of treating others as they want to be treated and considering how it would feel to have the same thing happen to them over time helps your child learn to stop and think and then hopefully act differently before repeating a misbehavior. This is also a great question to ask in general, for instance, while reading books, because it will reinforce how important you think it is to consider other people's feelings in addition to mastering one's own!

Read with feeling. Books are excellent vehicles for building vocabulary, literacy, and active listening skills and for improving *emotional* literacy. Even babies can read emotions on faces, which is why they tend to respond well to books featuring faces. When reading together, be sure to point out characters' emotions, helping your child learn to look for and become skilled at recognizing a wide range of them. As your child's understanding of other people's feelings grows, ask feeling questions about characters in books, like, "How do you think that little boy feels?" or "What do you think the little duck was feeling when he couldn't find his mother?" Finally, take advantage of the many children's books written specifically about feelings. As you look for books to share with your child, consider what each illustrates with respect to not only WE Skills but also all the other QI Skills. (See Appendix 1 for a representative list of popular children's books conveniently categorized by QI Skill to get you started.)

Sing, sing a song. The children's song "If You're Happy and You Know It" is popular for good reason. Not only does it offer a simple tune, plenty of repetition, and a catchy rhythm that encourages active enjoyment but also it provides a great way to introduce, reinforce, and have fun teaching your child about emotions. When you sing and act out the simple verses with your child, you reinforce (and put words to) the concept of being happy, what a happy face looks like, and that faces in general are important for conveying emotions. But you don't need to stop there. Take the opportunity to introduce other motions and emotions. Swap out clap your hands for stomp your feet, and happy for sad. Then try surprise and so on. Make up as many faces as you like, and as your child catches on, let her be the one to suggest new, more challenging emotions to act out.

6

QI Skill 3

WHY

Seeing the World as a Question Mark

> The important thing is not to stop questioning.
> Curiosity has its own reason for existing.
>
> —Albert Einstein

FIRST BABIES COO. THEN THEY babble. From there, the words start flowing. It takes surprisingly little time from when children utter their first, eagerly anticipated words to the point when parents (and everyone else) can expect to be besieged by a single, highly significant, yet at times parentally exasperating word. If you're thinking that the one particular word I'm referring to is "no," that qualifies as a reasonable guess in the context of toddlerhood, but one to save for a different discussion. No, the word I'm referring to, as evidenced by the title of this chapter, is *why*. This ubiquitous and ever-so-frequently repeated three-letter word is added to just about every three-year-old's vocabulary, yet it represents something much bigger and much more important than just a word tacked on to a toddler's growing vocabulary list or a challenge to parental authority. It represents the fundamentally important act of questioning that forms the core of our third QI Skill: WHY.

The Five Whys

A FEW YEARS BACK, I stumbled across a popular training technique first developed by an engineer at Toyota called the *Five Whys*. Well known to the business world, the Five Whys is an "iterative question-asking technique meant to promote deep thinking through questioning."[1] True to its name, the technique typically involves asking "why" five times for the purpose of getting to the root of problems and finding meaningful answers. Why five? Well, apparently that was the number originally deemed sufficient, but it's worth noting that it has since been recognized that asking even more "whys" in some instances proves to be beneficial and is therefore encouraged.

By encouraging and facilitating exploration of cause-and-effect relationships, the Five Whys continues to be a highly popular technique, adopted or adapted in various forms by many of the world's most innovative companies as part of their training regimens (including Kaizen, lean manufacturing, and Six Sigma, to name a few).[2, 3] From a business standpoint, this certainly seems straightforward enough, and makes good sense. Yet, ever since learning of the Five Whys, I have been bothered by a single, unanswered question of my own: Why should we have to go to such great lengths to train adults and high-level businesspeople, no less, to do something that anyone who has ever spent any time with a two- or three-year-old clearly knows occurs predictably, persistently, and naturally?

This question got me thinking. If it's asking lots of questions that we ultimately value, then perhaps we should dedicate some time to figuring out just what it is that seems to be training the WHY out of our children.

What Is WHY?

ON THE BASIS OF OUR discussion thus far, you might think we could just define WHY Skills as the asking of a fairly simple question and call it a day. But there's actually more to WHY Skills than meets the eye. As a QI Skill, WHY actually involves asking all sorts of questions about how the world works. It's a demonstration of inquisitiveness and curiosity in myriad forms. Asking *how, what, who,* and *when* as well as *why* falls under this skill's umbrella. As such, WHY Skills represent the fundamental thirst for knowledge and understanding that enables our children to figure out the world around them. And, as we'll explore in the chapters to follow, WHY Skills drive WILL, WIGGLE, and WOBBLE and ultimately facilitate WHAT IF—the ability to question at a deeper, more creative level and explore and question not just how the world is but also how it could be.

The Unquestionable Need for Inquiring Minds

TO UNDERSTAND WHY NOW MORE than ever our children are likely to benefit from having well-developed WHY Skills, it helps to take a look around and consider what has changed in the world since we were growing up. After all, it was only a couple of decades ago when access to what was then considered vast amounts of information came in the form of a complete set of the Encyclopaedia Britannica or as the result of browsing through the card catalog at the local library. Nowadays, it comes in the form of a connected device—a smartphone, tablet, or computer—and as a result of simply browsing the World Wide Web.

The ever-so-significant shift from an industry-driven economy to the sharing economy based squarely on information and knowledge we discussed in WHY NOW marks this striking period in history we happen to be experiencing firsthand. Technology, computerization, mobile access, and the rise of the Internet have also fueled this shift. We simply can't disregard the fact that we are raising our children smack dab in the middle of a virtual information revolution.

In fact, in a world where a week's worth of the *New York Times* contains more information than the average seventeenth-century citizen encountered in a lifetime,[4] it's easy to see how, like us, our children risk experiencing unprecedented information overload. We must ask ourselves what it means to raise children in a world of 24/7 access, where any bit of information imaginable is available in the flash of a Google search. Faced with this daunting task, here is the case for why cultivating our children's WHY Skills is so important.

Questions versus Answers

FOR OUR PURPOSES AS PARENTS, the profound shift from Industrial to Information Age has had and will continue to have significant implications for how we raise our children for success, not the least of which is recognition of the plummeting value of memorizing static facts and knowing the right answers and the increasing value of being able to ask and pursue answers to the "right" questions.

In one sense, we've always valued the questioning "reflex." We've long claimed "there's no such thing as a stupid question."

Albert Einstein himself is credited with saying: "If I had an hour to solve a problem and my life depended on the solution, I would spend the first fifty-five minutes determining the proper question to ask, for once I know the proper question, I could solve the problem in less than five minutes."[5] Yet it's one thing to say we value questioning, and another thing entirely to put this belief into practice.

In a world with challenges of mounting complexity, from climate change and fossil fuel shortages to revolutionary technologic change, healthcare evolution, and transitioning business environments, fostering the ability to ask good questions—and lots of them—is paramount to devising great solutions.

Take creativity, for example. With the value of creativity at an all-time high, recognizing that creative thinking requires asking great questions, rather than just reciting answers, should strengthen our resolve to foster our children's foundational WHY Skills. So should the fact that "curious people" are in high demand. A representative article in *Harvard Business Review* titled "Why Curious People Are Destined for the C-Suite" cites a study of a thousand CEOs in which respondents identified curiosity (along with open-mindedness) as a leadership trait that's gaining importance in these challenging times.[6] Being curious naturally involves WHY Skills and the ability to ask probing questions. As Dell founder Michael Dell has said, "Curiosity can inspire leaders to seek out the fresh ideas and approaches needed to keep pace with change and stay ahead of competitors."[7]

It isn't surprising that questioning—recognized as central to so many valued twenty-first-century skills—has become a prominent theme in business, leadership, entrepreneurship, and, of course, innovation. Consider LinkedIn founder Reid Hoffman, who has identified one of the defining features of entrepreneurs as "the constant asking of why." In the same vein, globally acclaimed businessman and philanthropist Ratan Tata recognizes innovators' inherent need to "question the unquestionable," and famed Harvard Business School professor Clayton Christensen notes that innovators are consummate questioners who show a "passion for inquiry."

In fact, based on the results of Christensen's six-year study of how people come up with groundbreaking ideas, he singles out questioning as one of five key "discovery" skills and concludes that what all innovators have in common, "in their DNA," is that they constantly ask provocative questions that push boundaries, assumptions, and borders and "leave few rocks unturned."[8]

With such a high premium being placed on questions over answers, on constantly asking why, on passion for inquiry, on leaving no stone unturned, on questioning the unquestionable, the conclusion seems obvious: anyone who values innovation, entrepreneurship, creativity, or curiosity or anyone simply hoping to raise their children to be successful in a knowledge-based world, WHY Skills are unquestionably essential.

Treating the World as a Question Mark

WHAT DOES IT LOOK LIKE when young children treat the world as a question mark?[9] In theory, it sounds fabulous: a young child eager to explore and learn, toddling around touching, tasting, pointing, and asking, "Why?" and "What's that?" In reality, however, it also involves that ever-so-eager child getting into everything and questioning rules, instructions, and requests in a way that can easily affront our parental authority and control.

When eBay founder Pierre Omidyar recounts, "My learning process has always been about disagreeing with what I'm being told and taking the opposite position, and pushing others to really justify themselves," it's easy to applaud him for his persistent questioning, given the business success he has achieved by doing so.[10] If, say, a four-year-old in a prekindergarten class-room were to employ the same approach, however, I'm fairly sure this same discovery skill—so highly valued in today's world of disruptive innovation—would not be quite so lauded. It might even land said four-year-old in a corner for a time-out. Simply put, the questioning of authority and the status quo doesn't fit well with our longstanding image of parenting, preschool, or well-behaved children.

When I think of how parents often view the notorious frequency with which young children use the word "why," I'm reminded of a quirky little porcelain figure of a chicken given to me by a family whose children were patients in my pediatric practice. This chicken perches on a shelf in my office and invariably draws a laugh from those who see it. That the chicken is a garish neon pink surely contributes to the reaction. But what is even more likely responsible is what's printed in chicken scratch on the sign the chicken holds, which reads: "Raising children is like being pecked to death by a chicken."

For anyone who has raised or spent any time around young children, it's not hard to understand why this admittedly exaggerated proclamation leads to chuckling. It's just so easy to relate persistent pecking to real-life parenting and, in particular, to being questioned and asked "why" ceaselessly by our offspring to the point of our absolute exhaustion. We, as parents, tend to respond to this exhaustion by defaulting to pat responses such as "because I said so." Such responses, though, eventually can discourage children from questioning altogether.

The Problem with "No Questions Asked"

AS A PHRASE FIRST POPULARIZED in the early 1980s by First Lady Nancy Reagan, "Just say no" quickly gained popularity and was widely applied as a national strategy to discourage alcohol and drug use among our country's youth. It's easy to understand why these three words received such fanfare. They were quick, catchy, easy to understand, and conveyed in no uncertain terms what we wanted our children to do (or, rather, not do).

Better yet, this was an approach that parents were comfortable with. There was just one little problem. Because "Just say no" robbed school-age children of the opportunity to learn how to thoughtfully and critically question and discuss a touchy topic, this popular no-questions-asked strategy was found to have little to no impact on the war on drugs.[11] Similarly, one could argue that it's not such an effective overarching strategy for the parenting of young children either, as excessive use of the phrase "Just say no" also risks diminishing development of WHY Skills in the early years.

I imagine right around now many of you are thinking, "Surely there's still a place for the word no!" And, in fact, there is. Even before young children start questioning the world around them using words and sentences, they do so by exploring. If a child is toddling toward danger, such as the edge of a pool, an electrical outlet, or a busy intersection, there's clearly a compelling reason to yell a loud and decisive "NO!" with no further explanation needed (at least not in the moment). In instances such as when a toddler questions what would happen if she were to stick something in an uncovered outlet, you can appreciate her inquisitive nature while also quickly and decisively ensuring that finding the answer is not left up to firsthand experience.

But in instances where the answer (or rule) isn't so clear-cut, take the time to consider whether you really want or need to discourage your child's questioning and exploration or whether it's simply a knee-jerk response you can work to deprogram as you come to appreciate the role your child's curiosity will play in fostering WHY Skill development.

Default answers of "because I said so" and "no" happen to be but two of the many potential obstacles to WHY Skill development that we, as parents and caregivers, need to rethink if we truly want to foster rather than squelch "question thinking" right from the start. Think about how tempting it can be to use any of the following responses when faced with persistent questioning:

> *Because I said so!*
>
> *No!*
>
> *Just do as I say!*
>
> *Follow the rules!*
>
> *Stop asking so many questions!*

All have become part of today's standard parenting lexicon. And, to a certain extent, they play a necessary role especially when it comes to following important rules.

Sure, it's easy to revere Steve Jobs and others who built their renown, in large part, on their predilection for not just questioning the rules but breaking, disregarding, and rewriting them. But when we're talking about young children, we must make sure they understand the rules and learn how to follow them, especially when said rules are in place for good reasons, such as for health or safety or to help them learn to play well with others and master important ME Skills. At the same time we must also allow them to retain their ability to question the world around them.

This admittedly poses a parental challenge: teach and enforce rules or encourage their disregard? Punish or praise children who continually question the rules? Practically speaking, achieving a safe and healthy balance while effectively fostering WHY Skills is entirely possible. In his interview with *The Atlantic*, Wharton business school's top-rated teacher Adam Grant, author of *Originals: How Non-Conformists Move the World*, refers to this balancing act as a Goldilocks effect. He points out that "too much structure, order, and discipline can constrain creativity, but so can too little."[12, 13] What it takes to get it just right is a good understanding of child development, a clear picture of your ultimate parenting goals, and, of course, a bit of parenting finesse.

Starting with WHY

BEFORE CONSIDERING OUR PARENTAL ROLE in protecting our children's early WHY Skills, let's first take a look at some of the common developmental milestones of early childhood that serve as the earliest signs of evolving WHY. Although this QI Skill lacks clear milestones conducive to being listed in a formal, age-based bulleted list, it is possible to sketch a developmental progression that will hopefully help you identify and facilitate your child's budding abilities in this arena.

Even before young children can demonstrate their verbal WHY abilities, it is apparent that they are intensely curious knowledge seekers by nature. Their inquisitiveness and WHY-like search for answers start when they're very young, even during infancy. Long before they can utter the word "why," babies and toddlers achieve a whole host of developmental milestones that represent early WHY Skills in the making. They develop unspoken questions about how the world works, and they get their answers by observing us. Nine-month-olds are developmentally able to start using their fingers to point at things in a handy sort of precursor to "what's that?" Although their lack of language skills may limit them from forming a well-worded question at this young age, rest assured that they are nonetheless intensely curious and focused on what you and others around them say and do to satisfy this curiosity.

Beginning around age one and all throughout toddlerhood, children start learning words, naming familiar objects, and exploring how these objects work. As parents, we're usually happy to supply them with answers to their "identification" questions. We understand the value of knowing the names of things and so are happy to increase their vocabulary and provide them with a basic grasp of the world around them. Early on, toddlers' questions are relatively straightforward, so it's easy to be pleased and entertained by their curiosity and quick to satisfy it.

And then the WHY Skill milestones really kick in. Children make a fairly obvious leap from toddlers posing their very first rudimentary query to five-year-olds who understand cause and effect and believe there is (or should be) a reason for almost everything and who consequently pummel you with questions.

As you've probably noticed, my initial WHY references focused on children between the ages of two and three years, and for good reason: this is the age at which young children really start to develop the brain power (and the underlying executive function skills) it takes to make logical connections between things. These sorts of cognitive leaps enable them to begin to understand why things happen. As a result, their innate inquisitiveness and curiosity predictably present themselves in full force in the form of questions. Lots and lots of questions. Young children want more and more information, and their developing WHY Skills serve as their chief source of getting it.

Of note, this age at which kids' cause-and-effect wheels really start turning also tends to signal the start of what is often referred to as the "age of independence," or, in some cases, the "terrible twos." After all, knowing how you think the world should work and then it not working out that way, or not knowing how the world works and getting frustrated that you can't yet figure it out, or lacking the verbal ability to ask specific questions and understand the answers might just make you throw a fit every now and then as well.

So, there you have it: the responsibility of helping children develop and retain their earliest WHY abilities rests squarely on our parenting shoulders. We are also responsible for striking a balance between making sure kids develop a healthy respect for the way things are and know how to follow rules, on the one hand, and making sure they never give up on questioning, on the other.

Questioning: Our Role as Parents

IT MAY BE ONLY NATURAL for young children to question the world around them, but what happens next is, in large part, up to us. After all, learning to put one's WHY Skills to work in a positive way takes plenty of support and encouragement.

I've found that one of the most helpful attitudes parents can adopt to cultivate their children's WHY Skills is this: consider it your child's *job* to ask questions and (in short order) to question limits, while also recognizing that it's your job to actually set some. The fact of the matter is that, starting with eating, sleeping, peeing, pooping, and playing, babies and very young children have only a few fundamentally important jobs to do. Questioning you and everything in the world around them happens to be among the most important. I've found that simply adopting this attitude helps to change our parental expectations as well as the way we respond to our children. After all, it's much harder to get irritated by our children's persistent questioning of us, our instructions, and our rules when we simply recognize they are doing their job and constructing the foundation of their WHY Skills. Recognizing that it is your job to nevertheless set some limits suggests that the rules you set and the answers you give should be well thought out and serve a purpose beyond simply exerting authority.

In the spirit of getting you off to a good start, the following are some general approaches and activities to help you foster your child's early WHY Skill development and strike this delicate balance between engaging their inquisitive minds and setting limits.

Start out answering unasked questions. Even with newborns, it helps to remember that talking is teaching, and you are your child's first and sure-to-be-best teacher. Given just how early the foundation for WHY Skills starts developing, don't wait until the day your child actually starts asking you questions to realize she sees the world as one big question mark. Rather, you can assume she's interested in whatever you have to say, and make it a habit to have fun simply narrating what's going on in the world around her—pointing out things of interest, naming things, and sharing your thoughts and insights as you go about your day together.

Ask questions of your own. Thoughtful questioning is a skill you want your child to see as lifelong. Well before children are old enough to ask *why* themselves, model for them how it's done by making it a point to let your child see you as a lifelong learner, someone who is always inquiring, asking questions, and being interested in figuring out how the world works.

Praise questions, not just answers. This one is relatively straight-forward: the more you respond to and appreciate your child's curiosity and questions, the more likely he is to continue asking them. This can be as simple as saying, "What a great question!" or making clear to him that his question is important by setting aside any distractions, giving him your full attention, and showing that you're dedicated to discussing the answer (and not just reading a result off of Google or Wikipedia and going about your business).

You can also take this a step further and ask, "That's an interesting question. What made you think to ask it?"

Gradually increase your Q/A ratio. The Q/A ratio represents the number of questions (Q) someone asks relative to the number of answers (A) that person gives.[14] Given what we now know—the importance of questions over static answers—it stands to reason that questions eventually should ideally outnumber answers. As parents, it's common to find our children turning to us for all the answers. Admittedly, it's nice to be seen as all-knowing, even if only in the eyes of a toddler, but it's important to realize that helping our children learn to make their way in the world involves helping them learn how to find their own answers. On the one hand, this ultimately means learning to curb our parental instinct to give our children all the answers. On the other, it's important to remember that young children, especially in the first few years, need answers to their questions in order to build their knowledge and vocabulary base. Figuring out how many answers to give depends on a child's age and abilities. I clearly remember the day when my daughter (then a toddler) repeatedly asked "what's that?" as we walked along the sidewalk, first pointing to a bush, then a car, then the sky, a bird, a bike. . . . Her questions (or, rather, her single question directed toward anything and everything around us) was an amazing display of a toddler's budding WHY Skills that required no prodding. It was also one that deserved just as many answers for a young child just learning the vocabulary. In contrast, as my children got older, I had to resist my urge to simply give them answers to all their questions and instead encourage and help them figure out how to find answers for themselves.

Be sure to teach WHY manners. The challenge of having a child ask lots and lots of questions isn't simply a matter of overlooking the inherent value of WHY Skills. More often than not, it also has a whole lot to do with when, where, and how the questions are asked. Interrupting, not taking time to listen to the answer, or asking questions at inopportune times all tend to describe toddler tendencies to a T. As you encourage your child to keep asking questions, be sure to also engage her ME and WE Skills of impulse control and awareness of others so she also learns to take turns, raise her hand, refrain from interrupting (a skill that can take quite some time to master), and listen attentively to what others say. At the same time, commit to carving out some daily "WHY time" when your toddler can ask questions to her heart's content and you can better appreciate her indefatigable questioning abilities—whether during dinner or drive time, at bedtime or book time, or simply while taking a walk or playing together.

Beware of discouraging questions. Research suggests that the two biggest inhibitors of adult questioning are not wanting to look stupid and not wanting to be viewed as uncooperative or disagreeable.[15] It's therefore worth considering when, why, and how we as parents (and other early childhood caregivers) typically *discourage* questioning. It's easy to come up with a list of common reasons: when we have our own agenda, when we're short on time and just want our kids to do something without having to answer lots of questions about it, when we don't know the answers ourselves, and when we interpret our children's questioning as an affront to our parental authority. Whatever the specific motivation, it's important to recognize this sort of reasoning as a common obstacle to encouraging our children's WHY Skills. Instead, remember to first ask yourself whether or not your child's questioning is truly out of line. Also, do your best to significantly limit your use of discouraging WHY responses such as "because I said so" and "no!" When used excessively, these sorts of answers may save you time and the need for explanation, but they will make it all too clear to your child that questions really aren't welcomed.

Turn to the pages of books. As you've probably noticed, reading books to young children can be a way to promote just about all of the QI Skills. With respect to WHY, books allow you the fun, practical, and endless opportunity to expose your child to all sorts of new ideas, pictures, and concepts that expand your child's worldview and understanding of how the world works. To encourage questioning, be sure you allow time to stop reading and let your child point at pictures, ask questions, and even flip back and forth to particularly intriguing pages or pictures rather than simply focusing on reading straight through, start to finish. Also feel free to jump in and ask your child an occasional thought-provoking question, starting with the simple find- or name-the-object variety and progressing to questions that probe deeper about the story.

7

QI SKILL 4

WILL

Self-Motivation:
Applying the Power of WILL

You can motivate by fear and you can motivate by
reward, but both of these are only temporary. The
only lasting thing is self-motivation.

—Homer Rice, former American football
player, coach, and college athletics
administrator

I N 1930, A NEWLY MINTED Stanford PhD psychologist named
Harry Harlow set up shop at the University of Wisconsin and
soon thereafter established an eponymous research lab that is
still in existence today.[1] In the decades that followed, Harlow and
his colleagues, along with a colony of rhesus monkeys, achieved
international renown. Working off the recognition that human
and monkey minds are of similar complexity and development,
they provided significant insights into social behavior, learning,

and developmental psychology.[2] In fact, they carefully conducted what would come to be recognized as landmark studies that, to this day, inform our understanding of how the social WE Skills develop, from infant attachment (or the lack thereof) to the development of affection and normal social relationships.[3,4] But that was not Harlow and his monkeys' only significant contribution to our understanding of QI Skills.

Motivation and Monkey Business

ONE PARTICULAR STUDY HARLOW CONDUCTED shed new light on the existence of a different QI Skill. The study itself was relatively straightforward: he gave his monkeys a contraption requiring three distinct steps to open, and then observed to see whether they could figure it out. The results were simple enough, as the monkeys learned how to operate the contraptions quickly and easily. What was more notable, however, was that each monkey did so *independently*, without any urging, teaching, or rewards from the researchers. Problem solved? Well, yes, and no.

This observed monkeying around with puzzles might not seem terribly surprising . . . that is, unless you take into account prevailing beliefs of the time. As Daniel Pink recounts in his *New York Times* best-selling book *Drive*, scientists of Harlow's time believed there were only two main drivers of behavior: those that were biological in nature (in other words, to satisfy hunger, thirst, or sexual appetite) and those that were based on rewards and punishments.[5] Yet neither of these two standard drivers of behavior explained why Harlow's monkeys mastered the task. After all, no monkey rewards had been given (which, in monkey experiments, typically involve food or affection). Making the results all the more puzzling was the fact that when subsequently offered rewards, the monkeys' performance actually dipped.

As you might imagine, Harlow and colleagues were left scratching their heads, wondering what, exactly, was the driving force behind the monkeys' unrewarded yet seemingly purpose-driven behavior. The answer is our next QI Skill: WILL.

What Is WILL?

WHEN MY THREE CHILDREN ENTERED kindergarten, each was officially inducted into an all-inclusive club their elementary school principal had aptly dubbed The Can-Do Club. Even before any sort of explanation of club membership was given, the name alone made it clear that this was a club to which I and—it's fairly safe to assume—all parents would want our children to belong. The club focused on recognizing its young members for their hard work, effort, and giving it the ol' college (in their case, kindergarten) try. I realized that committing to belonging to a Can-Do Club, in reality or in concept is, in fact, something to which we should all aspire. In relation to the QI Skills, this concept of a Can-Do Club (or attitude) also captures the essence of WILL Skills.

You can probably guess the many other related traits that characterize WILL. Included on this list are all of the highly valued get-the-job-done, go-getter, and stick-with-it attitudes. WILL is also well represented by the combination of commitment, conscientiousness, determination, gumption, persistence, perseverance, and focus put into action. WILL Skills are highly dependent on ME Skills because they inherently require attention, focus, and self-control. And when we look to the very heart of WILL, we find motivation.

WILL in a World Full of Carrots and Sticks

ON THE ONE HAND, THERE'S extrinsic motivation, the type of motivation that involves performing an action or behavior in order to receive an external reward or to avoid punishment. Those in the business of parenting or caring for young children might already be jumping ahead to the implications of this last statement as it relates to, say, rewarding toddlers with treats for a job well done, displaying sticker charts for good behavior, or promising dessert in exchange for one more bite of broccoli. Hold those thoughts for a moment because we're definitely going to get there, but first a little background.

The traditional approach of using extrinsic rewards to induce desired behaviors, also known as the "carrot-and-stick" approach, has long been utilized by the business world to incentivize desired workplace behaviors. Simply picture a horse with a tantalizing carrot dangling in front of its nose for the purpose of motivating forward movement. As for the stick? Well, that's for when the horse does not behave . . . you get the picture.

Business organizations and other fields have long relied on carrots in the form of bonuses, salary increases, perks, and other benefits to "encourage" employees to perform well. On the "stick" side of the workplace equation, poor performance reviews, censure from bosses, demotions, and terminations have all been employed as negative sanctions—the threat of these punishments working alongside rewards to keep employees in line and their noses to the grindstone. In short, this time-honored, twentieth-century, Industrial Age carrot-and-stick method of motivation has long served as a mainstay.

Yet what we now know about this method is that it rarely motivates people to go above and beyond or to forge ahead when others give up. That's not to say that carrots and sticks can't be motivating and promote efficiency, especially in the short term and for relatively monotonous, repetitive, assembly-line-type tasks. However, an abundance of research both in business and in psychology tells us that, going forward, relying on carrots or sticks simply won't suffice. In today's complex world that demands creativity and critical thinking skills, the motivational effects of extrinsic rewards simply don't last. Worse yet, in the long run they can actually de-motivate adults, monkeys, and, yes, even children.

As one of the most widely recognized authorities on motivation, Pink's highly informed assessment of the situation in his book Drive suggests, "Too many organizations—not just companies, but governments and nonprofits as well—still operate from assumptions about human potential and individual performance that are outdated, unexamined, and rooted more in folklore than in science."[6] He points out that these organizations continue to pursue practices such as short-term incentive plans despite mounting evidence that such measures usually don't work and often do harm. Worse, he says, these practices have infiltrated our schools, where we ply our future workforce with gadgets, coupons, and even cash to "incentivize" them to learn.

I share Pink's concern that our systems lag in updating our motivational methods to match our current understanding of the ineffectiveness of relying on extrinsic rewards. This, in turn, suggests that the parenting world has some updating to do as well.

Motivation from Within

NOW THINK BACK TO HARLOW'S monkeys. What Pink credits Harlow's monkey experiment with bringing to light was the other, previously unrecognized and powerful driver of behavior we now know as intrinsic motivation. This recognition of an inner force or "drive" (the latter term popularized by Pink) is captured in his summary description of Harlow's results: "The monkeys solved the puzzles simply because they found it gratifying to solve puzzles. They enjoyed it. The joy of [accomplishing] the task was its own reward."[7]

Evidence for the power of intrinsic motivation as a key driver of behavior was not contained in Harlow's monkey cages for long. Making the important leap from monkeys to humans, psychology graduate student Edward Deci challenged research subjects of his own—this time in the form of university students—with a different puzzling task. As it turned out, his human subjects also showed the same "inherent tendencies to seek out novelty and challenges" and to "extend and exercise their capacities, to explore, and to learn."[8] As a result, intrinsic motivation was on its way to becoming recognized as a key aspect of human nature, and the offering of external rewards (in Deci's experiments, money) was coming to be recognized as potentially detrimental to the development of intrinsic motivation in the long run.

Setting Our Parenting Sights on WILL

YOU MIGHT BE THINKING THAT all of this is fairly straightforward. After all, you'd be hard pressed to find even one parent who didn't embrace the idea of having their child grow up self-motivated with a can-do attitude, confident in setting and pursuing long-term goals, and conscientiously striving to achieve his or her personal best. So far, so good, but it's not quite that easy. There are a couple of parenting inconsistencies we need to address before we can make the strategic goal of fostering our children's WILL abilities a reality. The first is the prevailing attitude toward strong-willed children. The other has to do with M&Ms.

On Being Strong-Willed

IN LIGHT OF ALL WE'VE discussed in this chapter, being strong-willed surely is a good thing, right? It's a trait that seems to fit perfectly into the adult world's view of determination, perseverance, and the whole host of WILL Skills we've been discussing. Yet when these two descriptors are paired up with the word "child" in parenting circles, as in "strong-willed child," they have a different connotation, one that implies challenging with not-so-subtle undertones of "troublesome," "problematic," and "difficult." We may very much want our children to have strong WILL Skills in concept; in practice, it can be a bit more difficult.

Will Pee for M&Ms

THE OTHER PARENTING INCONSISTENCY BECOMES obvious as soon as we try to explain the phrase "Will pee for M&Ms." For those not familiar, this phrase refers to the common tactic of using M&Ms (or any treat) to reward potty-training kiddos who successfully manage to put their pee or poop in the potty. If toddlers and preschoolers were able to put crayons to cardboard and spell out their own demands, I imagine we'd see this phrase scrawled on signs outside little boys' and girls' rooms all across America (not unlike the "will work for food" signs that sometimes show up on our city streets). This and all of the other "if you do this, I will reward you" approaches to getting young children to do, act, and behave as we want them to have become so pervasive that we hardly recognize we're doing them anymore. Sure, a few M&Ms now and then for a job well done can seem relatively harmless and like a small price to pay. And, yes, rewards often work.

But it's worth thinking beyond the short-term celebration of no more diapers to what we're doing to our children's expectations. In short, we need to consider whether this transactional approach to parenting is necessary, and even more importantly, what unintended harm it may be doing in the meantime. Singling out potty training as a particularly good example, if ever there was a task for which mastery could and should serve as its own reward, one could easily argue potty training would be it. After all, freedom from wearing peed-in or poopy pants really should be reward enough. Of course, the same could be said of eating, sleeping, and so many of the other day-to-day tasks we're routinely and, in many instances, unnecessarily conditioning young children to expect rewards for. I fear that by doing so, we are teaching them early and often to expect rewards for any and all jobs well done.

Avoiding the Mitten Trap

EVEN WHEN WE'RE AWARE OF just how common the use of extrinsic rewards is in our current parenting culture and in the lives of our youngest children, it's all too easy to unintentionally fall right back into the extrinsic reward trap. The following is how it happened to me.

One of my favorite activities at the two-hundred-student educational childcare center I owned was our annual mitten drive. We were committed to helping young children learn about empathy and kindness and get early hands-on QI Skill experiences. Students as young as two years of age would bring in mittens to donate locally to those in need. Toddlers and preschoolers would dash up to me, pull mittens from their pockets, and proudly proclaim, "I brought mittens!" Parents fully supported our efforts, recognizing the value of encouraging their children to think about others, do good, and actively develop their WE Skills.

During this mitten drive month, teachers would help the preschoolers make tally marks to keep track of how many mittens each classroom collected. As the total number grew—typically reaching as high as seven hundred pairs—so did the children's excitement. One day, a member of my well-intentioned management team asked me whether we could reward the classroom that brought in the most mittens with a pizza party. Caught up in the celebratory sentiment, I agreed. It was not until well after the fact that I realized I had just turned an activity that was successfully providing intrinsic feelings of pride and accomplishment into one that offered extrinsic rewards. Instead of encouraging the warm and fuzzy pride of doing something nice for others, I had effectively shifted the reward from sharing mittens to eating pizza.

I, like many parents, made this shift with good intentions and failed to anticipate the counterproductive impact it might have on WILL Skills. After all, a good old-fashioned friendly competition sounds motivating and may well yield a higher number of mittens. In the end, however, it chips away at children's opportunity to experience the satisfaction of doing something for its own sake. Kids who are conditioned to perform for extrinsic rewards risk failing to develop the inner drive or flow that produces innovation and breakthroughs, especially in challenging tasks. Just as important, if they lack intrinsic motivation, they will never experience the deep fulfillment and happiness that comes from doing something well for its own sake—from hobbies to relationships to careers.

It's easy to rationalize extrinsic motivation, especially during the most demanding years of parenthood: anything that gets kids to do what we want and need them to do seems like a good thing. But, given what business and social science tell us about the potential for unintended consequences, we should be concerned that the cumulative effect of rewards can crack the foundation of our children's developing WILL Skills.

The Developmental Milestones of WILL

SO, WHAT DOES WILL LOOK like in young children? If you stop and think about it, early childhood is full of examples of WILL because it serves as a driving force behind the determination that enables kids to try over and over and over again. Take babies, for example. Over months and years they persist in cooing, babbling, and imitating their way to the ultimate goal of talking until they're finally able to be understood and effectively communicate. And we certainly see WILL in the "do-it-myself" determination of two-year-olds who attempt to dress themselves or who insist on brushing their own teeth.

No discussion of WILL Skills would be complete without mention of the classic and inspirational children's book *The Little Engine That Could*.[9] From the Little Engine's "I think I can, I think I can, I think I can" to its realization of "I thought I could, I thought I could, I thought I could" and associated feeling of accomplishment, this is the track we should hope our children will learn to follow. It's worth noting, however, that in today's parenting world, the Little Engine could just as easily end up on a different track depending on how we, as parents, approach our role. A cartoon recently shared on my Facebook page captures this cautionary note particularly well. A little engine sits idling, stuck at the base of a mountain. Rather than "I think I can," this little engine says, "Push me! . . . MOM! . . . Well? I'M WAIT-ING!" The caption reads, "The little engine whose parents did everything for him."[10]

Developing WILL Skills:
Where There's a WILL There's a Way

NOW FOR THE GOOD NEWS: The way we interact with our children really can be transformational rather than so heavily dependent on the "if-then" transactional approach characterized by peeing for M&Ms. One of my very frequent reassurances for parents faced with the assertive or "willful" child has thus been to remind them that, if cultivated in thoughtful and productive ways like those recommended below, the very same assertiveness and determination that can admittedly prove a tad bit challenging at age three will likely serve their child well at age twenty-three.

By thinking through your long-term parenting goals and purpose and the kind of "little engine" you want your child to grow up to be, you can start to be more intentional in building a strong foundation for your child's developing WILL Skills. In the end, we know that children who grow up learning the WILL Skills necessary for self-motivation and how to set and follow through on their goals are the ones likely to do better in life.[11] We also now know that, in general, the best place for carrots is not dangling in front of our children but on their plates, while sticks are best left to the great outdoors to be marveled at on nature walks.

Before we discuss activities to help you develop your child's WILL Skill foundation, however, allow me first to acknowledge that it's likely impossible to avoid rewards and punishments altogether. Occasionally resorting to a sticker here, a delayed bedtime there, or even a few M&Ms every now and then is no reason to beat yourself up. The key, as with so many aspects of life, is moderation. If you commit to limiting how many times you employ them, you're not likely to rob your child of self-motivation, determination, or grit. Only when it becomes a parenting pattern does it start to erode this QI Skill.

With that in mind, here are some key strategies you can use to strengthen and support your child's WILL Skills:

- **Avoid engaging in if-then parenting.** Knowing all we know about the long-term demotivating potential of (or dependency on) external rewards, limit your use of extrinsic rewards for jobs well done. This doesn't mean don't celebrate. Just be judicious, avoid making every task a conditional if-then-driven achievement, and make your child's self-motivation and pride in his "work" the focus of your celebration. After all, supportive affirmations that help your child start to recognize and feel a sense of accomplishment for a job well done, like, "I'm so proud of your effort" and "You should be very proud of yourself," over time serve to build WILL far better than sweet treats.

- **Model self-motivated behavior.** As Nobel Prize–winning economist James Heckman says, "Motivation begets motivation."[12] Similarly, in her book *Mind in the Making*, author and work-life researcher Ellen Galinsky asserts that adults foster children's motivation by being motivated themselves.[13] In a practical sense, this may involve allowing your child to see you participating in activities that you enjoy and from which you derive satisfaction (rather than just doing work or tasks for which you're rewarded). It also means demonstrating to your child the importance of sticking with tasks and seeing them through to the end even when they start to get boring, frustrating, or more involved or effortful than originally anticipated.

- **Resist swooping in.** We know WILL involves self-motivation. It also involves stick-with-it-ness. This means we need to allow children both the opportunity to try things for themselves and the time it takes to persist in accomplishing their goals. Whether it's a six-month-old reaching for, scooting toward, or trying to roll to an out-of-reach toy, a nine-month-old trying to pull to a stand, or a three-year-old insisting on doing everything "all by myself," recognize the WILL that drives these behaviors. When your child persistently and messily attempts to use a spoon, force yourself not to automatically take over. When your toddler sloppily attempts to drink from a cup, instead of reverting back to a spill-proof sippy cup, recognize the motivation—messy though it may be—for what it is. In other words, let your child figure out new stuff on her own as much as possible, even for relatively minor tasks that take a lot of persistence not to get bored and quit. I have long asked parents the question, "Who's driving the bus?" to help them recognize when they're inappropriately letting children have too much control (allowing them to throw a tantrum, for example, until they get to eat chocolate chip cookies for dinner). In the context of fostering children's self-motivation, however, we also need to consider whether we've gotten in the habit of taking over the wheel too quickly and too often before our children stand a chance of applying their own natural drive.

- **Anticipate an occasional battle of the wills.** As your toddler develops a mind of her own and increasingly applies her WILL Skills, it only stands to reason that doing so will occasionally lead to conflict with others. In fact, minor skirmishes are quite predictable when young children who are equally committed to getting what they want are put together and expected to share the objects of their attention. In general, conflict results simply because they haven't yet mastered the ME (self-control) and WE (relationships, empathy) Skills necessary to adjust their competing WILL-minded behaviors. It helps to keep in mind that, in essence, the same drive and determination with which young children refuse to wait their turn or return another child's toy, when applied in a more controlled and productive manner, will ultimately help your child succeed.

- **Prioritize perseverance.** Promote and praise age-appropriate stick-with-it-ness, trying hard, and persisting on challenging tasks. Let children know you appreciate when they help out with or complete monotonous tasks (like picking up stuff in their room). Recognize that younger children do have shorter attention spans, so what may seem like giving up in the context of an older child may actually represent an impressive effort for their age. For example, when a two-year-old keeps trying to build a tower of blocks for half an hour rather than five minutes, that's worth celebration! At a certain point, of course, it's fine to let them stop or to give them a hand, but you might just be surprised by how well they learn to persist, achieve success, and be rewarded with a positive feeling because they persisted when simply given the chance and some positive support.

- **Present them with puzzles.** It's no coincidence that researchers such as Harlow, Deci, and others use puzzles to test intrinsic motivation—the only reward subjects get is the satisfaction of doing and completing them. When left to their own devices, even very young children have proven themselves to be master problem solvers. You can find all sorts of puzzles for toddlers and preschoolers, from jigsaw puzzles with a handful of large pieces to basic video games that present a puzzle to be solved. Although you may have to encourage young kids to try these games or show them how it's done when they're just getting started, remember that they'll soon get the hang of it.

- **Take it slow.** We often unintentionally send children the message that we value quick and easy over effort (especially when that effort will take a long time). We tie their shoes when we're in a hurry instead of allowing them to fiddle with the laces for what seems like forever until they get it right. Obviously, at times we need to get somewhere or get the job done quickly, so we have to speed up the process. But whenever possible, give your child the time necessary to work at it and eventually complete a task. To develop WILL, kids need time.

- **Promote practice.** Keep in mind the old joke about a visitor to New York City who is hopelessly lost and comes upon a native New Yorker and asks, "How do you get to Carnegie Hall?" The New Yorker answers, "Practice, practice, practice!" It may on occasion seem dull, repetitive, and at times a bit endless, but practice is a great way for small children to develop their WILL foundation. It doesn't really matter what they practice, just that they stick with it over a period of time.

- **Give them goals.** If grit involves applying determination to reach long-term goals, then it stands to reason that we should help our children learn about and pick long-term goals. They can be in the natural form of mastering a new developmental skill, which children do very, very early when, for example, they really want to walk and keep trying and trying until they get it right. Or as they get older, learning to read, play on a team, or complete a puzzle. Start with reasonably easy-to-accomplish goals, but don't stop there: help your child build up over time to the sorts of goals that take more time, effort, and perseverance.

- **Pick up on passions.** Nothing helps young children to be motivated and commit to taking on tasks and setting stretch goals than making those tasks related to something they love. For babies newly learning to roll, motivation can come in the form of a toy placed just out of reach. For my toddler son (and all the way through age eight or so) his "driving force" (i.e., passion) was elephants. As an active toddler, he could enjoy listening to books for surprisingly long periods of time (hours) . . . so long as they featured an elephant somewhere in them. Fortunately, pachyderms didn't have to be prominently featured, just there. I quickly became an expert in locating books with elephants in them (bet you didn't know that even *Goodnight Moon* has an elephant within its pages![14]). Similarly, he was motivated to dress himself when elephants were featured on an item of clothing. You get the picture.

8

QI SKILL 5

WIGGLE

Putting Wiggles to Work

> Creative thinkers try new things and move with
> the changing world.
>
> —Elaine Dundon, *Seeds of Innovation:
> Cultivating the Synergy That Fosters New
> Ideas*

RECENTLY SAT DOWN TO WATCH the morning news and catch the lead stories for the day. First up was a story about parents in a Florida town who were protesting the elimination of recess in the local elementary schools. Sadly, this story wasn't the first of its kind; many schools struggle to meet rigorous national assessment standards and have cut recess as a way to create more time for academics. To my disbelief, however, the very next feature story was about the growing popularity of walking meetings and treadmill desks to help increase physical activity in the workplace. The broadcaster commented on how today's employers, increasingly aware of how beneficial getting up and moving can be to the overall health and productivity of the workforce, were implementing practical solutions to encourage such beneficial behaviors. The focus of this story, as with the one it followed, wasn't exactly breaking news either. In fact, the gist seemed to have entered our nation's consciousness more prominently a couple of years earlier when prominent Silicon Valley–based business innovator Nilofer Merchant presented her 2013 TED talk, "Got a Meeting? Take a Walk"[1] (which more than two million people have viewed to date), followed shortly thereafter by her *Harvard Business Review* blog in which she ominously but astutely declared, "Sitting is the smoking of our generation."[2]

Seriously? The striking disconnect between eliminating physical activity from our children's curricula while simultaneously working hard to incorporate it back into the workplace was jarring. I found myself cynically thinking about how employers could easily provide opportunity for employees' physical activity simply by using nearby elementary school playgrounds. After all, at the rate recess was being cut across counties, school facilities would soon stand empty and available. On a less pessimistic note, this juxtaposition convinced me it was high time we take a closer look at what we are—and are not—doing in our children's earliest years to encourage them to get up and get moving, not only for the sake of improving their health and well-being but also for their learning and future productivity.

That, of course, leads in to the fourth QI Skill, WIGGLE, which is about children's innate propensity to move and play as a way to explore their world and learn.

What's in a WIGGLE?

WIGGLE SKILLS DESCRIBE EXACTLY WHAT the verb "wiggle" suggests: the physical act of moving; being active; being in constant motion. Whereas moving and being physically active are essential elements of WIGGLE, they represent only part of the picture. Key to understanding the concept of WIGGLE is also recognizing that WIGGLE actually represents both physical *and* intellectual restlessness. Children's ability to physically move around and explore their world, starting from day one, is essential not only for their physical health and development but also for their cognitive development, learning, and ability to put their natural-born inquisitiveness into action.

You'd be hard pressed to dispute the fact that children learn through play. From the time they are infants through toddlerhood and beyond, play means a whole lot of motion—shaking rattles, stacking blocks, knocking them down, picking up toys, putting them down, rolling balls, opening drawers, closing them, crawling, cruising, climbing, pulling up, and engaging in countless other activities that seldom involve sitting still. When given the opportunity, children quite literally WIGGLE their way through childhood.

Albert Einstein said, "Play is the highest form of research." When it comes to active play, young children are experts, and our job as parents is to provide them with plentiful opportunities to move rather than to squelch their innate WIGGLE tendencies. Therefore, it's essential to redefine this sort of constant motion and restlessness of early childhood as exactly that: a lifelong skill to be appreciated, encouraged, and cultivated.

How the World Views WIGGLE

IF THIS CONCEPT OF LEARNING and motion going hand in hand still seems a bit abstract, take a moment to think about how often we use action words to describe ideas, goals, and cognitive abilities: we appreciate those who cognitively take baby *steps* or big *leaps* forward as moving in the right direction; we recognize the need to allow for *wiggle* room in both a conceptual as well as a physical sense; and we actively encourage setting *stretch* goals and *reaching* for the stars. Successful entrepreneurs are admired for their *hustle* and are described as being in constant *motion*. We recognize *movers and shakers* as people who get the job done, we place high value on *agility* (the ability to move quickly and easily), we acknowledge those who *rapidly* iterate, and we cheer on those who *take action*, are *active* listeners, and so on. In short, if the way we talk about both physical and intellectual restlessness is any indication, we clearly value WIGGLE Skills in the adult world and the professional arena.

The Mind-Movement Connection

PHILOSOPHER HENRY DAVID THOREAU IS credited with making the mind-movement connection in the nineteenth century, having noted, "Methinks that the moment my legs begin to move, my thoughts begin to flow."[3] In the 1960s, researchers started more concretely establishing this connection between physical fitness and performance on cognitive tasks. Since the 1990s, researchers have been building support for the belief that being physically active doesn't just improve our physical health but also boosts our ability to think more clearly and creatively. For example, a 2014 Stanford University study found that walking heightened creative inspiration by an average of about 60 percent.[4]

Having dedicated much of his professional career to researching this mind-movement connection, Harvard psychiatrist and best-selling author John Ratey has found that physical activity inherently prepares learners by conferring a host of benefits that extend well beyond physical health and well-being: from improved ME Skills (impulse control, behavior, and attention) and WILL Skills (motivation) to valuable improvements in mood, anxiety regulation, and self-esteem. All of these are attained through exercise and simply getting up and moving.

How, exactly, physical activity bolsters brainpower isn't entirely understood, but it is the subject of significant interest and inquiry. In 2015, researchers in Switzerland published a study in the journal *Brain Plasticity* that found mice that ran on wheels developed twice the normal number of new neurons and showed improved abilities on cognitive tests afterward.[5] Other studies have found that stepping away from your computer to move your body, such as going for a walk, replenishes your energy, which improves your focus, concentration, creativity, and productivity when you return to work.[6]

The reality is that, although the body of research explaining this complex body-brain connection may still be in its toddlerhood, it is growing quickly. And what is already clear is that aerobic physical activity has positive effects on cognition and brain function at the molecular, cellular, system, and behavioral levels.[7] Allowing children to develop their WIGGLE Skills, starting in their earliest years, is essential for creating a lifelong habit of using the body to move, learn, and discover.

WIGGLE While You Work

APPLICATION OF THESE MIND-MOVEMENT FINDINGS is making its way into today's world of business and innovation, where walking meetings and treadmill desks are but two of the many WIGGLE-building activities rapidly being introduced, appreciated, and embraced. Even the ubiquitous Ping-Pong, pool, and other game tables found on the floors of every start-up company are credited with generating creativity and productivity—not hindering it.

In *The Innovator's DNA*, Harvard Business School professor Clayton Christensen makes the point that innovators rarely sit still. He draws a parallel between physical and intellectual restlessness: "Experimenters unceasingly explore the world intellectually and experientially, holding convictions at bay and testing hypotheses along the way. They visit new places, try new things, seek new information and experiment to learn new things."[8] In other words, what innovators seem to all have in common is that they're constantly out investigating the world around them—something that would inherently be difficult to do if you weren't allowed to move around in it. This statement holds equally true for infants, toddlers, and preschoolers.

All of this adds up to an all-out WIGGLE movement that is gaining momentum as more and more employers are becoming convinced that physically moving increases employees' focus, attention, creativity, and energy for improved output. Armed with these insights, we shouldn't be surprised that, in a variety of work environments, exercise equipment for employees is installed; coworkers and CEOs alike engage in walk-and-talk meetings; benefit packages include fitness club memberships; and free or discounted wearable activity trackers are offered to employees as are training and executive development regimens that involve physical challenges. Not to mention more and more cubicle walls are coming down in favor of open floor plans so that employees can move about and more easily "run into" each other and engage in face-to-face collaborations. People are no longer expected to sit at desks all day, at least in progressive organizations that recognize the value of WIGGLE. And it's not uncommon to walk into a meeting and find a handful of small, colorful toys or objects strategically placed on the table so that attendees can toss, stack, fiddle, fidget, and otherwise play with them. These "manipulatives," as they're called, are not set out simply for entertainment or distraction but as an intentional effort to keep participants engaged by allowing their bodies to keep moving so that their creative juices keep flowing.

A WIGGLE by Any Other Name

NOW, CONSIDER FOR A MOMENT the language we commonly use to describe active young children. We say "fidgety," "antsy," "restless." I was recently introduced to the Yiddish word shpilkes, which does a similarly good job of conveying how those of us responsible for keeping up with young children typically view their impulses to move and explore, touch new things, and test out all sorts of ways of interacting with the world around them. Shpilkes literally (or at least in a "see also" sense) means "ants in the pants," the inability to sit still. Most of the time, it is an expression a parent directs at a child who seems to be bursting with nervous energy: "Can't you sit still for even a second? You've got the shpilkes!"

In contrast to the twenty-first-century adult world that now embraces WIGGLE Skills, in the parenting world young children's tendency to be in constant motion is often viewed as something that needs to be limited, controlled, or contained. In other words, a distinct undertone of undesirability tends to surface whenever we talk about our toddlers in motion. Let's face it, you're unlikely to ever hear a parent wistfully proclaim, "I wish my child were more fidgety," or proudly report on their child achieving a new level of "antsy-ness." And even the alternate definition of shpilkes as "impatience" or "agitation" has a distinctly negative connotation.

We have come to accept the picture of a "well-behaved child" as the calm, quiet kid who sits still and doesn't reach, touch, grab, poke, or otherwise get into things. Rather than embracing free and active play to be the work of three-year-olds, we're mistakenly accepting the definition of "work" as synonymous with "seat work," which obviously must be done sitting down. At best, we treat any sparks of restless energy as something we need to extinguish, sort of like removing the batteries from an Energizer Bunny.

Given these attitudes toward WIGGLE—which, I argue, are not just semantic—it's not surprising that some parenting mindsets tend to play out in ways that work against developing our children's WIGGLE Skills early.

WIGGLE Restrictions

SO, WHAT, EXACTLY, IS STANDING in the way of our children's earliest WIGGLE development (aside from our general attitude toward it)? One, if not the most pervasive, WIGGLE-prohibitive practice facing young children today is what I refer to as our "strapped-in" mentality. Consider all of the many items we use on a daily basis during our children's earliest years to keep them buckled down and restrained: car seats, strollers, bouncy seats, stationary activity centers, baby carriers, swings, high chairs, booster seats . . . the list goes on.

As a pediatrician and a mom who juggled three kids very close in age, I can't discount the fact that each of these items serves a very useful purpose, most importantly, safety, along with soothing, feeding, transporting, playing, and protecting. I'll be the first to acknowledge that I couldn't have survived those early years without them.

Where I fear we've shown an overabundance of restraint, however, is in allowing ourselves to sit back and become overly reliant on our ability to shift babies and young children from one strapped-in device to another. As a result, they have little opportunity to roll, scoot, and crawl. Our toddlers are left with little time to toddle (or WOBBLE). And our preschoolers are afforded less time to actively play, explore, and discover. Our broad adoption of this strapped-in approach to parenting significantly limits our children's opportunities to move around and work on their WIGGLE and other QI Skills. What starts out as practical necessity becomes skewed too far toward parental convenience. For example, we strap babies into swings or high chairs instead of setting them down on baby mats or blankets while we prepare our meals; we use strollers to get around with our children faster and easier long after they are more than capable of hoofing it themselves.

These defaults restrict children and teach them early on to passively watch the world go by because they have no opportunity to engage it. For a three-month-old, there's obviously no viable alternative to being carried or pushed in a stroller to get from point A to point B. But for a three-year-old, there is. If children are rarely given the chance to test out their sea legs, to WIGGLE in a physical sense and interact with their environment because they are always being restricted in one way or another, their WIGGLE development runs the very real risk of being stunted. Though it may go without saying, this strapped-in mentality also has huge implications for our children's future physical well-being.

Unfortunately, things don't look so good when it comes to providing our preschoolers with ample opportunities to WIGGLE. Having spent nearly a decade as the owner of a private preschool, I can tell you that the perception of a well-run classroom does not include nearly enough time and space to WIGGLE.

It's About Time to WIGGLE

If you think cutting recess time in elementary schools seems like a valid cause for WIGGLE worry, consider findings from a University of Washington study involving preschoolers. Active play constituted a mere 12 percent of the study subjects' day, with the children playing outside an average of barely thirty minutes per day.[9] Napping accounted for nearly a third of their time, and the preschoolers spent the rest of their day eating or otherwise engaged in sedentary activities.

Sit Still and Listen

NOT TOO LONG AGO, A new mom of an eight-month-old mentioned to me how excited she felt that her baby was no longer just interested in trying to chew on books whenever she attempted to read to him. He was starting to sit in her lap and look at the pages while she read. She could even get through several books at a time! As someone who's always been passionate about reading aloud to young children—I especially loved reading to my own every night—I could absolutely understand her excitement.

However, her comment also jogged something else I'm passionate about: Why have we come to believe that reading must always be a stationary activity? Why, based on all we know about WIGGLE, do we picture an eager and engaged child, one who is truly ready to learn, as one who sits perfectly still, criss-cross applesauce, in a designated spot on a reading rug? One who doesn't fidget, move, or otherwise WIGGLE while listening to stories? Or, for that matter, one who keeps books out of his mouth? It's hardly this mom's or any parent's fault that we've come to believe that's the only way our children will absorb the stories we read. But when you take a moment to think about how much young children need to WIGGLE, holding on to this belief can be counterproductive if it means we won't read to kids unless they're still.

I'd even go so far as to suggest that handling and chewing on books are some of the earliest precursors of literacy. To become proficient in a skill down the road, children first must be interested, curious, and engaged. For infants, this means using their mouths and hands, the WIGGLE tools they have available, for exploring. When viewed in this light, the idea of gumming the corners of a book as an antecedent to literacy doesn't seem so outrageous. From there, toddlers learn to hold the book, turn the pages; then they discover there are words on those pages, and before long they realize those pages contain stories that one day they can read themselves. Fortunately, someone really wise created durable board books so that we can and should feel comfortable allowing even babies to handle and explore books in the WIGGLE ways that come so naturally to them.

When my children were young, I literally read hundreds of books to them each year, yet—I feel the need to add this—that by no means implies they sat perfectly motionless on my lap as we turned page after page. Rather, often I would read while they played, crawled, colored, and otherwise WIGGLED attentively nearby—quiet activities that helped keep them engaged with the stories much longer. They would stop what they were doing to eagerly turn their attention to the pictures. Meanwhile, I knew that they were absorbing the vocabulary and stories in the books, not to mention enjoying the shared activity of reading as much—if not more—than if they were sitting perfectly still with me.

So, Where Does WIGGLE Start?

AS EVERY PARENT INVARIABLY DISCOVERS, young children have the impulse to move and explore, to touch new things, and to test out all sorts of ways of physically interacting with the world around them, an impulse that frequently keeps us on our toes, especially in the first few years of our parenting lives. This ability and drive to WIGGLE actually starts remarkably early. With a kick, jab, twist, or turn every now and then, babies routinely remind their pregnant mothers (as well anyone else who has ever been invited to place a hand on a pregnant belly) that they can't wait to be set free from their snug uterine confines and begin exploring the world.

Once born, newborns also demonstrate their WIGGLE prowess in impressive ways. Within hours, newborns placed on their mothers' chests possess both the WILL and the physical ability to WIGGLE their way up to their mothers' breast to nurse. This impressive newborn WIGGLE-ability, first described by Swedish researchers in the late 1980s and later by one of my pediatric mentors, John Kennel, and his colleague Marshall Klaus, captures the innate nature of WIGGLE. As they noted, this newborn "Breast Crawl is associated with a variety of sensory, central, motor and neuro-endocrine components, all directly or indirectly helping the baby to move and facilitate her survival in the new world."[10]

In the late 1970s, internationally renowned baby brain researcher Andrew Meltzoff also demonstrated newborns' amazing (not to mention endearing) ability to combine WIGGLE and WE when he described their ability to stick out their tongues in response to an adult doing the same.[11] Not only is this simple physical act of imitation enough to amaze and entertain proud new parents, it also reveals just how incredibly responsive babies (and their brains) are to social interaction and learning to WIGGLE in the outside world from day one.

Wired to WIGGLE

WE NOW HAVE EVIDENCE OF babies' intriguing ability to WIGGLE that is not always visible to the naked eye. That is, unless you have the eye of a baby brain scientist and happen to be equipped with some powerful brain imaging technology. In the late 1990s, Italian researchers using electrodes to monitor brain activity in monkeys were the first to focus on a special type of brain cell called "mirror neurons," which humans are believed to possess as well. These intriguing brain cells have been shown to fire not only when an individual performs an action but even when he or she watches *someone else* perform the same action.[12]

Considering this concept in relation to the WE Skill of learning to master language, Dr. Patricia Kuhl (you may recall from WHY EARLY that she is the preeminent early language and brain researcher based at the University of Washington's I-LABS in Seattle) has conducted landmark research that suggests that babies actually *practice movements* in their brains long before mastering them physically. Using cutting-edge neuroimaging technology, Kuhl witnesses what happens inside babies' brains as they watch and listen to someone speak. In the areas responsible for the motor movements required for speech, she has found that these areas in babies' brains are activated simply by hearing adults speak, well before these babies coo, babble, or master speech movements themselves. What this baby brain research tells us is that not only are babies wired to WIGGLE but also they do it for very good reasons.

The Motor Milestones of WIGGLE

LET'S MOVE ON TO THE actual movement part of WIGGLE—the standard "motor milestones" of early childhood—that most parents clearly recognize. Even before they're born, babies WIGGLE in utero. Infants WIGGLE as they discover their hands and feet. Toddlers WIGGLE all day long. We can see that they are born "restless," and we have access to a whole lot of information about just what normal development looks like when it comes to being physically active. Because they are key aspects of WIGGLE, it's worth quickly reviewing the typical time line of important motor milestones from birth onward:

- **Newborn:** Born with a whole host of involuntary reflexes, newborns have little intentional control over anything more than basic movements. That said, some can lift their head a bit to take a look around, and it's only a short time before their increasing muscle strength allows them to move more.
- **Two months:** Still not showing many outward signs of constant motion, two-month-olds can typically hold up their heads and they start pushing up when lying on their tummy. Movements of the arms and legs at this age become smoother and more controlled as babies gain control over involuntary reflexes.
- **Four months:** Babies at this age begin taking control of their movements. Four-month-olds characteristically reach for toys with one hand, coordinate hand and eye movements, hold their heads up high and steady, push up onto their elbows when lying on their stomach, bear down on their legs when feet are on a hard surface, prepare to rock, and then soon start rolling from front to back.
- **Six months:** Six-month-olds start to demonstrate their curiosity about things more physically. They make an effort to get objects that are out of reach, master the skill of rolling over in both

directions, begin sitting without support, and may even start to support their weight on their legs and bounce when supported upright. Some six-month-olds may start rocking back and forth and even scooting or crawling backward.

- **Nine months:** "Up and at 'em!" This is when babies start pulling up to a stand, stand holding on, and crawl (in all sorts of creative ways). Fine motor skills start to appear as well, as nine-month-olds can pick things up using their thumb and index fingers (known as the "pincer grasp"). This allows them the increased ability to explore, and also to end up putting things in their mouth. Nine to twelve months is also when you might start to see the earliest walkers starting to get up and go.

- **Twelve months:** Exploring at this age typically involves putting their well-developed shaking, banging, and throwing to good use. One-year-olds can generally get themselves to a sitting position without help and may even take a few steps without holding on.

- **Eighteen months:** This is the age that all but defines toddlerhood, as eighteen-month-olds perfect their toddling and become increasingly steady walkers. In some instances may even walk up steps or run.

- **Two years:** By age two, toddlers are typically off and running—actively searching for things (even when hidden), climbing, and going up and down stairs (while holding on).

- **Three years:** Doing the hustle accurately describes the motor abilities of three-year-olds. They busily and physically explore books, puzzles, and blocks; learn to work toys with buttons, levers, and moving parts; climb well, run easily, and get up and down stairs in a more coordinated way by placing only one foot on each step.

- **Four and five years:** Now able to hop, skip, kick, spin, throw, catch, and move forward, backward, up, and down with steadily improving agility, pre-kindergarteners are ready for all sorts of action—both physical and cognitive.

Let the WIGGLE-ing Begin!

LIKE MOST QI SKILLS, DEVELOPING your child's WIGGLE Skills is often more about giving them the space, time, and encouragement to WIGGLE than having to actively facilitate. Left to their own devices, even newborn babies naturally practice their WIGGLE Skills. They are wired to do so, and they will squirm, and these squirms will evolve into more active and intentional movements: rolling, scooting, crawling, cruising, walking, and running.

We need to recognize that young children and adults alike absorb knowledge and develop strong QI Skills when they're in motion. Sure, letting your child WIGGLE more will likely require a bit more thought, safety-proofing, time, and supervision, but in the long run it's well worth it. Rather than simply working to get their WIGGLES out, our role as parents should therefore be to help them put their WIGGLES to work. Here are some ways you can help them do just that:

Recognize WIGGLE when you see it. As simple as it may seem, recognizing that physical and cognitive learning go hand in hand is a big step in the right direction when helping your baby develop this important skill. Now that you know what to look for, you can appreciate your child's early attempts to WIGGLE for what they are. Perhaps your infant will discover her hands or reach for a toy hanging from her activity gym for the first time. These activities are just as fascinating for her as they are for you. Whereas these early WIGGLES are easy to appreciate, be sure to continue to remind yourself of the value of WIGGLE as your child becomes more mobile, increasingly gets into things, and, as a result, keeps you on your toes throughout the day.

Swaddle with care. Swaddling, by definition, generally involves wrapping babies in a blanket or cloth. Although there are permutations, swaddling generally includes wrapping arms, legs, and all, and doing so fairly snugly so that babies' natural reflexes won't cause them to wriggle free. Swaddling is a popular strategy for calming babies and helping them sleep, and for good reason given its sleep-inducing results. That said, be aware that it also restricts WIGGLE. Now that you're familiar with the benefits of WIGGLE-ing, it's important to avoid suppressing your baby's WIGGLEs when they're awake and active, lest swaddling go from being a way to soothe your baby and improve sleep to an early and overused form of restricted WIGGLE. Instead of relying solely on swaddling for daytime calming, turn to other effective methods for soothing your baby (such as singing or rocking) and reserve swaddling primarily for sleep.

Make time for tummy time. Chances are you know tummy time to be an important activity to prevent flat head syndrome, which can result from babies spending too much time on their backs. But tummy time happens to be very valuable for WIGGLE-related reasons as well. For infants, tummy time *is* WIGGLE time. When babies who are not yet able to roll, sit, or crawl spend awake time on their bellies, they have the opportunity to move and strengthen their head, neck, and body muscles while also taking in a new view of the world. You can facilitate this early form of exploration by simply making time for tummy time and, better yet, getting down on the ground and lying across from your baby so that you can interact face to face. Also look for opportunities to allow tummy time in new locations throughout your home and even outside of it (weather and location permitting).

Create plenty of WIGGLE room(s). Childproofing is essential for keeping young children safe at home and anywhere else they spend time. When a space is properly childproofed, it gives parents increased peace of mind so they can sit back and let children move and explore more freely. Finding and creating safe spaces where your child can do so is important not only for WIGGLE-ing but also, as you'll soon discover, for the WOBBLE-ing that inevitably follows. So, instead of considering all of those cabinet latches, baby gates, and outlet covers as ways of limiting your baby's activities, consider them a means for allowing *more* freedom and room in which to safely WIGGLE.

Allow for active reading. For children who find it hard to sit still—for toddlers and preschoolers, this can represent the majority—be aware that there are many things you can do to more actively engage them in reading. Try, for example, reading "active" books (some examples of which can be found in Appendix 1) and allowing children to get up and act them out as you read, miming the actions in books like *Jump, Frog, Jump!*[13] and *Wheels on the Bus.*[14] For others (my three children included), simply offering them the chance to quietly build puzzles, color pictures, create beaded crafts, or any of a whole host of other age-appropriate manipulative options may be more than enough to enhance their engagement with the story, not to mention their attention span, while also providing them with the opportunity to "fidget," move, and WIGGLE.

Beware of withholding WIGGLE. In light of all we know about the benefits of WIGGLE-ing, we should all think twice before deciding to withhold the opportunity for children to get up, move, and run around. Think about the preschooler who's not allowed to play outside because he wouldn't sit still and focus in the classroom. Unfortunately, it's not uncommon for fidgety, WIGGLE-y kids to be punished by restricting their activity, when the reality is that they are the ones whose focus and attention could likely benefit most from being given the opportunity to WIGGLE.

Run free. From the time toddlers learn how to pick up speed, parents seem to fall into the trap of routinely telling them, "Don't run!"—a cautionary command once reserved for "special" occasions (think: broken glass, busy streets, and other instances in which running actually poses a serious safety risk). In cases where it doesn't serve a clear purpose, the frequent use of this common parenting command runs counter to what we hope to instill in our children when it comes to WIGGLE-ing their way to success. As long as the surroundings are safe, let them run free! As a mom, child care owner, and pediatrician, I've seen my fair share of skinned knees and bitten lips that result when young children trip and fall. Still, the benefits of letting them run far outweigh the potential risks (which, most of the time, you'll be able to magically mollify with some TLC and a Band-Aid anyway). They'll learn, from a very young age, to use their body in new, productive ways, discover new things about how their body can move and rapidly change directions, and develop a whole host of skills that can later enable them to use more advanced WIGGLE Skills, such as playing sports and pursuing other physical endeavors.

Explore the great outdoors. Whether playing, running, taking nature walks, or simply collecting sticks, pinecones, or leaves, stepping outside your home provides limitless opportunities for simultaneously moving, learning, and exploring the world.

Beware the strapped-in temptation. Think about how much time your child spends in a car seat, stroller, bouncy seat, high chair, or other type of contraption that limits movement. These straps come with a price, limiting children's first and foundational abilities to move and explore. For all those times when safety isn't a concern, release them from these ties that bind. That means not using car seats to restrain your child at home, in the crib, or at the child care center. Once your child can walk, instead of pushing him in a stroller each and every time you go outside, make time for and encourage him to walk. Yes, there will be times when safety, time, or distance considerations will not allow it, but remember that the opportunity to take lots of baby steps inevitably leads to bigger and better things.

Change your preschool perception. If your image of a "perfect" preschool classroom has always been one involving calm, quiet, and orderly behavior, then hopefully you'll look at it differently now and consider adding some WIGGLE to this picture. Though there's a time for quiet and for sitting still, time for running and jumping and exploring is equally important. A good preschool should allow your child ample opportunities to do both.

Put WIGGLES to work. Playing active games such as Duck, Duck, Goose, Simon Says, and tag naturally encourage preschoolers to be physically active while learning. It also, as you'll recall, helps them learn to exercise a whole host of the other QI Skills, including ME, WE, and WOBBLE. Even young babies and toddlers can actively participate in simple WIGGLE games such as singing songs like Pat-a-Cake; Head, Shoulders, Knees, and Toes; and the Itsy-Bitsy Spider that link words with physical motions.

9

QI SKILL 6

WOBBLE

Failing to Succeed: Raising Children Who Are Fit to Fail

> Many people think you get stability by minimizing all risk. But ironically, in a changing world, that's one of the riskiest things you can do.
>
> —Reid Hoffman, *The Start-Up of You*

I N 1971, THE PLAYSKOOL DIVISION of the Hasbro toy company introduced Weebles. These popular egg-shaped and bottom-heavy toys came in a variety of styles but shared one defining feature: they could be pushed, tipped, and tossed, yet always return to their upright position. After more than forty years, more than a hundred different Weebles, and many millions of wobbles, this classic toy's catchphrase "Weebles wobble but they don't fall down" has remained embedded in the minds of generations of children as well as their parents.[1] That Weebles repeatedly tip, falter, and otherwise wobble yet reliably adapt is the defining feature of their success. It is this very same wobble-ability that serves as the foundation for this chapter's QI Skill: WOBBLE.

Being able to WOBBLE yet remain standing, in a figurative sense, represents a crucial ability today. Simply put, we need to embrace the risk of making mistakes and trying to accomplish new feats that are beyond our current capacities. In every type of organization and every endeavor, we recognize now more than ever the need for people who are willing to try out all sorts of new and daring ideas, falter, fail, and bounce back up, wiser and more resilient than before. Like the weight built into and anchoring each and every Weeble, the capacity to WOBBLE provides adults and children alike with a firm but flexible foundation. It helps them learn to embrace and rebound from failure; explore, adapt, discover, and innovate. The ability to WOBBLE well also facilitates the development of other foundational QI Skills, especially the WHAT IF Skills we discuss in the next chapter.

WOBBLE in Action

EVEN THOUGH MANY PEOPLE REMEMBER the "Weebles wobble" motto and the idea of WOBBLE-ing as a skill makes good sense in theory, many parents today struggle with putting this QI Skill in particular into practice and allowing much if any WOBBLE-ing to happen. As parents, we tend to be especially reluctant to let it happen at an early age. After all, what seems like a good idea in theory is admittedly difficult to watch (much less welcome) when it involves your toddler teetering, tipping over, and inevitably tumbling. Rather than recognizing WOBBLE as a valuable skill in the making and nurturing a child's natural willingness to test, explore, fall down, get up, and try again, we succumb to our current parenting culture—a culture that is caught up in the need to protect our children at all costs and from all forms of failure and upset, whether physical or emotional.

As a pediatrician, I'm the last person to discount the importance of injury prevention and "cushioning the blows" of early childhood; bike helmets, car seats, and always laying babies to sleep on their backs, for example, are highly recommended and extremely important safety measures. There's no question that we must continue to implement these sorts of measures to cushion kids from serious and potentially life-threatening, unrecoverable blows.

But we also need to seek balance in our approach. In *The Blessing of a Skinned Knee*, psychologist Wendy Mogul does just that, as she warns us against overprotective parenting and shares how some moms and dads bend over backward to prevent their kids from experiencing even the slightest stumble, scrape, or upset.[2] If this sounds familiar, keep the image of a Weeble in mind as a way to seek balance. Yes, we need to provide children with a safe environment in which to WOBBLE, but we also need to afford them the opportunity to fail early, fail often, and ultimately fail forward.

Before examining how to recognize, appreciate, and foster our children's earliest WOBBLEs, let's first consider why the ability to WOBBLE is proving to be such a valuable competency in the twenty-first century.

The Rise of Failure

FOR YEARS, FAILURE HAS GOTTEN a bad rap. In school, in business, in science, in politics, and in sports, tremendous value has been placed on "getting it right," while failure has been all but verboten. "Failure is not an option" is a phrase popularized by the 1995 movie *Apollo 13* that captures what has become a

concerningly pervasive sentiment. As a result, the more successful we are at dodging failure, the more we are recognized,
praised, and rewarded. Under these circumstances, it's no
wonder so many people are hesitant to take chances, unwilling
to test new approaches, take on new challenges, or tackle stretch
assignments for fear of appearing reckless or of messing up. To
advance in a world where WOBBLE-ing is perceived as a sign of
weakness, it's only natural to want to appear upright and strong,
sticking to and showcasing what we already know how to do.

But, as we know, things are changing and they're changing
fast. In large part, this is because recognition is growing that
failure is essential for innovation and that you can't innovate if
you're not allowed to fail. In recognizing this is the only way
we can solve the complex problems of today, a strangely intriguing trend has started to appear across the worlds of business,
entrepreneurship, leadership, and innovation: leaders, managers,
investors, and organizations are placing high value on the ability
to embrace and learn from failure and on those people best able
to do so. In response, companies are questioning twenty-first-
century job applicants about their past failures. Unlike in days
past, however, employers do not see these failures as black marks
on applicants' records but rather as positive—if not required—
signs that they have the experience necessary and are ready, willing, and able to take on challenges.

When we look around, the signs of this shift from valuing
"standing tall" to seeking out and prioritizing WOBBLE-ing are
everywhere. Of Google's nine stated Principles of Innovation, for
example, two are directly related to failure. Principle 5 stresses
iteration, encouraging employees to try lots of things "often and
early" without striving for perfection. Even more directly, Principle 8 states, "Fail well," acknowledging that to be innovative and
successful, failure should not come with a stigma, the environment should treat failure as a badge of honor, and people should

fail with pride.[3] And in his book *Work Rules!* Google's head of People Operations (a title, one could argue, that applies to each of us as parents) Laszlo Bock shares one of Google's key principles: the rewarding of thoughtful failure.[4]

Higher education has similarly followed suit. Aspiring college students are no longer asked to simply list their awards, grades, scores, and accomplishments and then allowed to rest on their laurels. Upon sitting down to complete the standard Common Application now used by a majority of colleges and universities, today's students are likely to find themselves faced with an essay option that reads something like this: "Recount an incident or time when you experienced failure. How did it affect you, and what lessons did you learn?" Once they enter college, they may even happen upon a course akin to "Failure 101," an actual engineering lab course that required students to take risks and experiment with an understanding that the more they failed, the better their chances of receiving an A in the course.[5] In short, failure has acquired a positive connotation, and the ability to fail has now become a sought-after skill.

Spaghetti and Marshmallows: A Test of WOBBLE-ability

PICTURE A ROOM OF PEOPLE divided into teams of four or five. Set on a table in front of each team is one large marshmallow, twenty pieces of uncooked spaghetti, a yard of string, and a yard of tape. Each team has eighteen minutes to build the tallest possible freestanding tower with these supplies; the ultimate goal is to build the tower to support the weight of the marshmallow placed on top with toppling over. What do you think typically happens in this situation? Who do you predict would be best at this spaghetti-marshmallow challenge? Before making your prediction, of course, you'll likely want to know two additional key pieces of information: whether the participants are adults or children and, if they're adults, what their professions are.

Now here's where things get really interesting, because even knowing the ages and professions of the participants, you might jump to the wrong conclusion. As it turns out, Tom Wujec, an Autodesk Fellow and globally recognized thought leader on creativity, design, and strategy, has orchestrated many such Marshmallow Challenge competitions, and what he has found in assessing the results is both striking and instructive: in fact, teams of recent *kindergarten* graduates on average perform particularly well at this tower-building task. Recent business and law school graduates, on the other hand, fare significantly less well. Even CEOs aren't able to outperform the recent kindergarten graduates. In fact, only two types of teams outperform the kindergarteners: engineers and architects (given the specific task at hand, no big surprise), and CEOs—but only if they have administrative assistants on their team.[6] So, what's going on? Why are young children better able to handle this complex assignment than so many highly educated and experienced adults?

Certainly WE Skills come in to play —teamwork, communication, and quick collaboration help teams complete the task successfully. As for the CEOs, one might speculate that they fare less well on their own because they tend to be better at giving directions than playing well with others. Or, as Wujec put it in his 2010 TED talk: kindergarteners don't spend time trying to be "CEO of Spaghetti Inc."[7] But there are far more than WE Skills at work in the process.

The business terms *rapid iteration* and *prototyping* describe the key abilities that young children display particularly well in this Marshmallow Challenge. Of course, this innovation culture jargon means nothing to kids (or most parents, for that matter).

But it should. That's because this Marshmallow Challenge helps us to more clearly see how young children possess an innate and eager willingness to try new things, to fail, to adapt, and to try again. And, yes—if this has you thinking back to WILL Skills, it should, as WILL-ingness is a necessary factor in making WOBBLE happen.

Consider that kindergarten kids make an average of five separate attempts to build their marshmallow towers during their allotted eighteen minutes. Contrast their efforts with newly minted MBAs who, on average, make only one marshmallow attempt—not surprising in that they've traditionally been trained to search for, find, and implement the one single right answer. As a result, when faced with an unknown and challenging task, they tend to spend most of their allotted eighteen minutes debating and drawing on preexisting assumptions, only to try once— and fail—to execute their "perfect" solution just before time runs out.

No doubt the MBAs and perhaps the CEOs, for that matter, want to avoid being perceived as uncertain and unsteady. They've been inculcated to believe that a "wobbly" leader is indecisive, weak, fickle, and likely to fall/fail. Yet as this marshmallow-spaghetti tower experiment demonstrates, winning teams WOBBLE their way to success. In a world with myriad options, rapid change, and ambiguous situations, WOBBLE is a much more useful skill than being single-minded, falsely confident, or fearful of failure. Now think about how many years, not to mention how much time, money, and effort, go into training the WOBBLE out of our "highly trained" business, legal, and other professionals; this counterproductive situation makes a very compelling case for why we need to look to early childhood and focus our efforts on protecting and cultivating our children's WOBBLE Skills.

The Developmental Milestones of WOBBLE (or Lack Thereof)

AS A FUNDAMENTALLY IMPORTANT QI Skill, WOBBLE turns out to be an anomaly in regard to developmental milestones. Unlike most other skills, WOBBLE lacks a clearly defined progression from one skill level to the next. That's because by definition milestones are measures of success, whereas WOBBLE-ing consists of all of the behind-the-scenes repeated failures and adaptations necessary to achieve them. Learning to WOBBLE is an ongoing process. Like today's rapid iteration approach of "aim, fire, aim, fire, aim, fire," it makes it inherently impossible to point to a successive series of specific goals achieved or competencies gained. Instead, from a developmental standpoint, WOBBLE Skills represent the *process* rather than the end result. As parents, we need to recognize the importance of this WOBBLE-y process and be sure to celebrate equally our children's WOBBLES as well as their ultimate milestone successes.

Now, that's not to say that young children aren't using WOBBLE Skills from the time they're babies, because they are: they are trial-and-error machines, trying, failing, adapting, trying again, and so on. Rather, it's children's innate WOBBLE-ability that ultimately leads them to eventual mastery of all the classic childhood developmental milestones, from holding their heads up and rolling over to pushing themselves up, crawling, walking, talking, and the list goes on.

If you're like many parents, you may run the risk of failing to fully appreciate much less celebrate and commemorate your child's WOBBLE Skills in action. This should be a concern, because if you fail to recognize the importance of (and allow for) all your child's many early failed attempts on the path to success, you run the very real risk of overprotecting, overcompensating, unnecessarily shielding your child from failure, and suppressing WOBBLE-ability. To avoid standing in the way of your child's budding WOBBLE Skills, you're going to want to focus on and celebrate the admittedly messier, more time-consuming, and less-than-orderly process it takes to master all other new skills.

Learning to Fail Forward

AS THE MARSHMALLOW CHALLENGE REVEALS, young children are quite adept at trying new things, failing, and adapting. The part that requires our parental support is actually allowing children to do so and helping them learn to fail forward. These two factors are key to the WOBBLE Skill development process as opposed to making children feel inadequate or slow because they're not mastering a particular task or ability; not recognizing their efforts if and when they fall short of a goal; exhibiting fear or concern because they tumble harmlessly; and simply focusing too much on getting it right.

Failing forward involves encouraging intelligent risk taking; offering verbal support for your child's ideas, efforts, and attempts regardless of specific outcomes; and providing opportunities for them to try and fail at all manner of activities. Recognize forward-failing moments for what they are and provide encouragement and support when they occur. Without this recognition, you may unintentionally respond to these failures with anxiety or, worse, discouraging words and actions. Keep in mind the mounting evidence that failure promotes learning and growth. The greater your awareness of your child's WOBBLES, the easier it will be to resist your overprotective impulses.

What Does Early WOBBLE-ing Look Like?

ALTHOUGH FOCUSING ON FAILURE DOESN'T exactly allow you to measure your child's development through typical milestones much less record them for posterity in any traditional baby book, you may recall my earlier point that failures and mistakes make other types of milestones achievable. So, what, exactly, does this look like in early childhood? Here are just a few of the many milestones that the willingness and ability to WOBBLE make possible for babies, toddlers, and preschoolers:

- **Self-feeding with a spoon.** Children don't typically master the much-anticipated milestone of spoon-feeding themselves with any real degree of accuracy until somewhere around eighteen months of age. That's not to say, however, they don't spend a whole lot of time trying, during which you can expect a lot of near-misses and at least as many spills and messes. My advice? Remember to celebrate (and even commemorate with a photograph or two) your child's blossoming WOBBLE Skills and the many unsuccessful attempts that in the short run are sure to leave food everywhere except the spoon's intended target.

- **Walking.** Learning to walk clearly involves a significant degree of WOBBLE-ing. Early attempts at mastery are invariably marked by trips and tumbles, as even the word "toddling" itself conjures up an image of a young child taking baby steps forward even though a fall is soon to follow. At nine to twelve months, some children spend more time on the ground than on their feet, while others—the early walkers—refuse to settle for simply pulling themselves to a standing position and toddling from one piece of furniture to the next. Instead, they segue straight from making it onto their feet to attempting to walk without relying on any cautionary steps, supports, or handholding. These particularly hard-core WOBBLERS insist on trying to walk, taking more than their fair share of tumbles, but more than willing to brush themselves off and try again . . . if only we let them.

- **Self-dressing.** The failures here are many and myriad (and often comically hard to miss)—mismatched socks, shoes on the wrong feet, odd pairings of shirts and pants, struggles with buttons and snaps. That's because when budding WOBBLE Skills cause children as young as two or even younger to *attempt* to dress themselves, a lot of amusing "errors" tend to take place over the several years before kids achieve independent dressing.

- **Saying the alphabet.** This is perhaps my favorite go-to example for encouraging parents to recognize and celebrate WOBBLE Skills in action. After all, we don't expect our five-year-olds to master the alphabet suddenly and without any trial and error. Rather, we start singing the alphabet to very young babies and enthusiastically encourage their attempts to imitate us. These attempts invariably start out as little more than mouth movements and coos, progressing over time to vaguely musical mumbles and slurred sounds that faintly resemble the names of the letters. Technically speaking, these early attempts could be considered failures. It can take years of such "failed efforts," struggling predictably with certain letters (*l, m, n, o*), putting them in the wrong order, saying them incorrectly, repeating some while leaving out others, before children's persistent WOBBLE Skills lead them to finally get it right.

Adult-Imposed Obstacles

AS PARENTS, WE TRY TO protect our children from the f words: fall, falter, fumble, flail, and fail. We do so out of love and out of a sense that this is our role—we want to keep our kids safe from anything that might cause them physical or emotional harm, and we want them to succeed by getting it right. To a certain extent, most of the other well-intentioned adults in our children's lives have the same objectives. Grandparents, teachers, nannies, and others all attempt to prevent or cushion falls and other types of failure.

What we all need to be aware of and collectively commit to, however, is creating an environment in which it is safe for our children to fail. We also need to adjust our perspective on what "failure" truly means. Instead of thinking about "failure" as not getting something right, we need to start seeing and directing it—especially as it pertains to young children—as WOBBLE-ing in the right direction. We must prioritize protecting against the crash-and-burn-type failures that are physically harmful or emotionally traumatic while also letting children get a few scraped knees and allowing them to experience a manageable degree of frustration or upset if they can't seem to keep their blocks from tumbling or their food from falling off of their forks, for example. The bottom line is that in a world that esteems, rewards, and requires fail-and-adapt skills, we owe it to our children to become more conscious of allowing them to develop their foundational WOBBLE Skills very early and throughout their childhood.

To foster this consciousness, let's look at some of the obstacles that often stop parents from allowing their children to WOBBLE:

Fear. Parental fear is good when limited to areas where real harm can come to our kids; it motivates us to protect them from things that can hurt them. The problem is when this fear of failure or danger spreads to areas where our children are actually at little risk, and we're doing much more harm than good. For instance, we see our child struggling with a toy and, rather than letting her figure it out for herself, we intervene, concerned because she has had a temper tantrum or seems upset or frustrated. We fear that she'll somehow be traumatized by her frustration. Similarly, we may set up all sorts of artificial boundaries to protect our kids but at the same time end up limiting their ability to explore and interact with the world. We become paranoid about everything from scrapes and bruises to insect bites and being exposed to other children's run-of-the-mill germs.

It's easy to understand how and why our protective parental instincts might kick in, but this reaction also brings to mind the "Bubble Boy."[8] Perhaps you read about or saw the movie about the young boy from Texas (David Vetter) who was encased in a big plastic bubble because he had a very rare disease that made him highly susceptible to infection—even catching a cold might, in his case, have been life-threatening. This condition not only left him without a functioning immune system but also created a huge WOBBLE-ing deficit. For him, even the smallest degree of risk taking could have been fatal. He couldn't interact with the world around him or enjoy any of the experiences we take for granted. Fortunately, most children are not afflicted with this condition. They do not need to live their lives in big plastic bubbles or fear the introduction of risk (common colds or otherwise). We should not deny our children the highs and lows, the successes and failures that are part of interacting with people, toys, nature, and the world.

I previously discussed parents' fear of letting their kids run in the context of WIGGLE Skill development, but it's a point that bears repeating here. You can't go to a playground or schoolyard or zoo without hearing an adult shouting at a preschooler: "Don't run!" Yes, don't let them run on broken glass, when they might topple over the edge of a cliff, or when they might veer onto a busy street. But, don't run *at all*? If there's nothing to fear but some scrapes and bruises from the occasional fall that comes with running—especially when one is a novice just starting out practicing the skill—then you have to curb your own fears and let them run. Sure, they'll fall at first. Some may even cry. But soon they will learn to jump back up, forget their tears, and join the pack of other kids zooming around the playground.

Need for control. Some parents simply don't like the uncertainty that comes with letting kids make their way in the world through trial and error, learning by doing, and adapting after failing. They feel as if their authority has somehow been diminished because they're ceding a measure of control to their children. Yet just as businesses have learned that the command-and-control leader is becoming a role of the past, parents would be wise to do the same. Many organizations want employees who know how to fail, who are committed to being agile, and who can learn by doing. This isn't going to happen if bosses (or parents) exert rigid control over every task and process. Adults and children alike need to be granted the freedom to WOBBLE. Parents must make a concerted effort to let go, at least to a certain extent. We can still maintain our authority if we switch our mentality from that of an authoritarian boss to that of a mentor and coach.

Taking failure personally. Many parents treat their children's mistakes and setbacks (as well as their successes, for that matter) as if they're their own. They feel as if they're not doing their job if anything, no matter how minor, "goes wrong" on their watch. This seems to be especially true of high-achieving parents who expect their kids to succeed at the same level as they did. These parents dislike how it feels to stumble, get the answer wrong, or fail, and they find it painful to watch their children experience it. On one level, this is a natural reaction—we instinctively want to nurture and protect, and so we want to shield our children from failure. Instead, we need to let kids develop self-reliance from an early age. We need to let them own their failures rather than viewing them as reflections of ourselves and our parenting abilities.

Competition. In today's parenting world, it often seems like parenting success is equated with whose child can roll, sit, babble, walk, or talk first, fastest, and best. This is what I call "the race through the milestones." It's unfortunate for many reasons, not the least of which is the emphasis placed on getting it right the first time, the fastest, and without any hint of failure. Yet no actual prizes exist for any of these races, and none of them is a predictor of how well kids will do in school or in life. From a WOBBLE standpoint, it's all too easy to find yourself entering your child in a false competition, wanting him to achieve milestones before his peers. You also may mistakenly focus on his achieving goals on the first try rather than on letting him fail, learn, and eventually succeed. If so, you risk encouraging him to limit his efforts to only those tasks he knows he can easily accomplish and to shy away from new or challenging activities, which defines a *fixed mindset*, researched and described by distinguished Stanford psychologist Carol Dweck in her book *Mindset: The New Psychology of Success.*[9] In contrast, encouraging children to embrace WOBBLE makes it far more likely they'll end up with what Dweck advocates as a *growth mindset*, one that welcomes new challenges and takes pride in the process of accomplishing them—WOBBLES and all.

Activities That Put WOBBLE Skills in Motion

TO FACILITATE A WOBBLE FOUNDATION, you can take a number of actions—and refrain from others—to help your child maintain and strengthen this incredibly important QI Skill. The goal is to create an environment in which your child can explore, test things out, and try lots of new behaviors without the fear of or serious repercussions from failure. The following are a sampling of activities that can help you achieve this goal:

WOBBLE-proof your child's environment. Otherwise known as safety-proofing, this activity is as much for you as for your child when it comes to cultivating WIGGLE and WOBBLE Skills, because safety-proofing children's surroundings helps protect them from serious injury with the added benefit of giving us the peace of mind necessary to step back and let young children explore. This calls for some common sense, placing padding over sharp edges and installing safety devices (such as plugs for electrical outlets), for example, along with some restraint, lest you find yourself padding the walls and wrapping everything in bubble wrap. At the same time, remember that a certain low level of risk comes with the WOBBLE territory.

Allow children to fail early and often. It's the *early and often* part of this prescription that is difficult to follow. Let's take learning to walk as a classic example. You may feel negligent as a parent if you simply sit back and watch your toddler repeatedly fall, especially if he happens to be the up-and-over type of new walker. Or perhaps you feel like you should go in and help your ten-month-old settle back down in the crib the first time he pulls to a stand in the middle of the night without yet having figured out how to lay himself back down to sleep. This is perfectly understandable, but when you make a commitment to tolerating an early-and-often recoverable failure regimen, you give your child the opportunity to figure things out for himself and in turn strengthen his WOBBLE abilities. Allow me to share a lesson I learned from my firstborn when she was learning to walk. Though she was a cautious toddler, she still had her share of tumbles as she tested her walking muscles. Occasionally, her falls would include what we referred to as a "head bonk." These are distressing but generally harmless knocks to the head. As a pediatrician, I knew the difference between a serious blow to the head and head bonks; the latter rarely cause any harm. As a result, my husband and I trained ourselves not to overreact as we might have otherwise—trying to prevent her from ever falling or running to her immediate rescue whenever she faltered—and instead taught our one-year-old daughter to brush off these head bumps (not to mention develop an early sense of humor) by saying "cuckoo, cuckoo." Here are two benefits if you choose to adopt a similar strategy: you accept psychologically and emotionally that minor falls and bumps are bound to happen and no real harm comes of them, and you help your child learn to brush off manageable failure and rebound, thus enhancing her WOBBLE Skills development.

Find the balance between risky and risk. Risky means allowing your toddler to play unsupervised near a busy street. Allowing for risk means encouraging your preschooler to climb an age-appropriate playground apparatus where she might fall—but where she's unlikely to suffer more than a bruise or scrape if she does. Thinking in terms of balance points provides parameters that can help you right-size your child's risks and keep her in the WOBBLE zone. Distinguish between unnecessary risks and risks associated with recoverable failure. Allow your child to experience those that are necessary, calculated, and lead either to recoverable failure or new learning and skills. Tossing aside bike helmets is clearly not the answer. But allowing your child to learn to ride a bike is.

Celebrate mistakes and failures. As parents, we tend to focus our greatest enthusiasm on successes and achievements—the first words, the first steps, and so on. What I suggest here is that you show similar excitement over noble but unsuccessful early attempts, failures, and adaptations in everyday activities from building blocks to coloring to speaking. Clap your hands, voice encouragement, and celebrate your child's persistence in the face of "failure" in other ways. I recently learned that my nephew's enlightened kindergarten teacher actually praises children's willingness to WOBBLE by having the class join her in cheering "hip, hip, hooray, we have a risk-taker in class today!" This sort of demonstrable support for efforts involving risk with a purpose goes a long way toward encouraging young children's lifelong willingness to WOBBLE. After all, you want your child to grow up recognizing that stability is going to come from adaptability, and making mistakes is not the opposite of success. Rather, learning from one's mistakes ultimately paves the way to it!

QI Skill 7

WHAT IF

Imagining a World of Possibilities

Children are the R&D department of the human species—the blue-sky guys, the brainstormers.

—Alison Gopnik, *The Philosophical Baby: What Children's Minds Tell Us about Truth, Love, and the Meaning of Life*

The creative adult is the child that survived.

—Ursula K. Le Guin, author

IN TODAY'S WORLD, WHERE WE live so much of our lives online and through social media, you don't have to look much further than how many likes, shares, views, or retweets an item garners to get a taste of what captures people's attention at any given moment. Now, consider TED—a global organization that hosts and then posts online talks covering an impressively wide range of topics. It's become known as "the world's largest stage."

TED's most watched video is one that over forty million viewers around the world have deemed an idea worth spreading (which, appropriately, happens to be the TED tagline). It's striking, not to mention refreshing, to note that the star of this "viral" video isn't a cat playing with yarn, a celebrity, or some random person performing a cringe-worthy stunt gone awry. Rather it's English author and international education adviser Sir Kenneth Robinson. The subject of his 2006 19.5-minute talk: "Do schools kill creativity?"[1] It's clear that his focus on creativity and what we are and are not doing to foster it in schoolchildren is of immense global interest and importance. It leaves little question that now, more than ever, we care about creativity—a lot.

Creativity is what the world needs. Remember that it has been estimated that 65 percent of the jobs today's first-graders will occupy don't yet exist and they'll be using tools to perform them that haven't even been invented.[2] The world has changed, and though I don't believe we need to raise every child to become a future entrepreneur, innovator, or CEO, there's no question that creativity will be essential for career success in just about every field in our "emerging creative economy."[3] Columnist for the Atlantic and acclaimed author of The Rise of the Creative Class Richard Florida notes, "Access to talented and creative people is to modern business what access to coal and iron was to steel-making."[4] Creativity is the raw material that will enable today's first-graders to invent, fulfill, and succeed in those careers that don't yet exist using the tools that have yet to be imagined.[5]

However, as Robinson warns, "Our education system has mined our minds in the way that we have strip-mined the earth for a particular commodity and for the future it won't service. We have to rethink the fundamental principles on which we are educating our children."[6]

Although Robinson's emphasis is on the education system, I suggest that it's not just the education system that will play a significant role in nurturing our children's creativity. It's us parents, and we have a responsibility that begins much farther "upstream" than our children's first day of formal schooling. As Robinson goes on to say, "I believe passionately that we don't grow into creativity, we grow out of it; or rather, we get educated out of it."

As will become much clearer throughout this chapter, it is in the realm of infants, toddlers, and preschoolers where WHAT IF Skills are born. That means that we, as parents, must play an even earlier role than schoolteachers in encouraging or squelching creativity. If we're successful at cultivating the seventh and final QI Skill, this incredibly important ability will survive and thrive well beyond the early childhood years of pretend, dress-up, and make-believe and offer our children a great advantage in today's world of innovation, creation, and self-invention. That skill, of course, is WHAT IF.

Little Hands, Big Imaginary Feats

IT'S A TYPICAL SPRING AFTERNOON. I walk into a classroom in my childcare center to find three prekindergarten students focused on an eclectic mix of toys that have been strategically placed in a pattern the significance of which is not immediately (or even remotely) clear. There is a box and a tower of wood blocks stacked almost as tall as those responsible for stacking them. As I attempt to step carefully across what could justifiably be perceived as one big mess, the architects of said "mess" quickly caution me to proceed no farther lest I find myself in grave danger. I am, you see, stepping into an imaginary world of space ships and evil villains, where the daunting task of saving the planet rests squarely on the shoulders of pint-sized, caped crusaders who are willing to attempt just about anything and who stand united in their shared belief that they will not fail.

This powerful, albeit messy, image of imaginative preschool play (also representative of the "mature make-believe play" we discussed in WHY ME that helps to develop strong executive function skills) is not just cute. It paints a picture of what it looks like to imagine the unimaginable and believe in endless possibilities—both highly sought-after skills that capture the very essence of WHAT IF.

What Is WHAT IF?

WHAT IF SKILLS ARE A core group of highly prized abilities that enable us to envision things in new and different ways from what currently exists. In other words, they allow us to think about, ask, and then act on the question "What if? . . ." WHAT IF is a skill that's most obviously about creativity, but it's also much broader, encompassing curiosity, imagination, innovation, open-mindedness, and out-of-the-box thinking. WHAT IF allows us to look at the world through the lenses of "I wonder . . ." "Imagine that," "What else?" "What would happen if . . . ," and "Why not?"

John Muir, founder of the Sierra Club, astutely noted, "The power of imagination [is what] makes us infinite."[7] WHAT IF allows kids to believe that not even the sky's the limit. Instead of operating within the framework of "You have to see it to believe it," WHAT IF is the ability to see opportunities and possibilities— not just problems—and believe that if you can imagine it, then you can create it or achieve it. As parents, we know this on a very instinctual level. We want our children to grow up believing that they can be anything they want to be: a scientist, president, doctor, dancer, zookeeper, programmer, business owner, and, yes, some days even a superhero. But what's so powerful about WHAT IF Skills is that they allow us to envision not only how our own lives could be but also the world as it could be. With WHAT IF, we can imagine a better world, and by drawing on all of the other QI Skills, as you'll soon see, we have the power to transform our visions into realities.

WHY versus WHAT IF

AT THIS POINT, IT MAY have occurred to you that WHAT IF and WHY sound similar; both are questions that are designed to probe for answers and generate new understanding. The biggest difference between these two skills is that WHY involves asking questions about how the world works to better understand the way it *is*, whereas WHAT IF involves questioning the way the world is to better understand and imagine how it *could be*. In short, WHY Skills inform us and give us the building blocks we need. WHAT IF Skills determine what we can create with those blocks.

One of my favorite quotes that gets right to the heart of why children need to know how to ask WHAT IF comes from Jean Piaget, the esteemed Swiss developmental psychologist, who poignantly asked, "Are we forming children who are only capable of learning that which is already known? Or should we try to develop creative and innovative minds, capable of discovery . . . throughout life?"[8] I believe that the answer to this question is the latter: as our children's first and most influential teachers, we owe it to them to actively develop their WHAT IF Skills.

Endless Possibilities

AS I'VE NOTED ON A number of occasions, all the QI Skills are intricately interconnected and facilitate one another. What sets WHAT IF apart is that it is the QI Skill that ties all of the other individual skills together. Without ME, WE, WHY, WILL, WIGGLE, and WOBBLE, it would be difficult, if not impossible, for children (or adults, for that matter) to be creative, to innovate, and to conjure up fresh possibilities, much less have the skills or drive to act on them. To sum it up, it's a strong sense of ME combined with the collaborative foundation of WE and driven by motivational WILL that allows children to ask WHY and WIGGLE their way through a world that embraces WOBBLE so they can learn to ask WHAT IF and create opportunities that will ultimately improve their own lives and the world around them.

Like WHY and all of the other QI Skills, WHAT IF is innate. Even the youngest of children naturally examine the bewildering and intriguing world they're in and start to ask WHAT IF? And it's up to us to encourage them to continue asking. After all, the world needs people who are skilled in more than following orders. We need individuals who are masters of reinvention, who can dream up and bring to life ideas that no one ever imagined before. And we need them not just in traditional creative fields and jobs; we need them in all fields. The obvious goal, then, is to find ways to nurture and develop these WHAT IF Skills.

More Than OK—Creative OK

CREATIVITY ISN'T JUST ABOUT INVENTING the next Uber, Facebook, or iPad; it isn't solely relegated to the innovation culture of Silicon Valley; and it doesn't rely on the investments of venture capitalists. Creativity is about solving problems, making people's lives better, and moving our communities forward. As such, it is recognized as a powerful necessity for generating solutions to some of the world's most critical economic and societal problems.

A movement aptly called Creative Oklahoma serves as an impressive example of how nurturing and developing these skills is starting to occur on community and state levels. Creative Oklahoma is a nonprofit founded on the belief that bolstering the state's current and future economic success will be achieved by boosting the creativity of its citizens. The organization's mission is simple yet profound, to establish Oklahoma as a world-renowned center of creativity and innovation that fosters these skills through initiatives that cross all realms, including early childhood education, the arts, the workforce, and the community.[9]

As a member of a global creativity network dedicated to advancing creative and entrepreneurial culture, Creative Oklahoma hosted the 2015 Creativity World Forum. I had the opportunity to attend this event where, not surprisingly, Sir Ken Robinson was a featured speaker. Something he said struck a chord about why we all should care so much about creativity. To paraphrase, he said that what defines us as humans isn't just our opposable thumbs but our ability to imagine things that don't yet exist.[10]

Creativity is at the heart of who we are, and we want to see it develop to its fullest capacity by fostering it as early in life as we possibly can. LinkedIn's Reid Hoffman echoes this sentiment when he writes, "All humans are entrepreneurs . . . because the will to create is encoded in the human DNA."[11]

Putting WHAT IF to Work

IN A GLOBAL SURVEY OF more than fifteen hundred CEOs, respondents identified creativity as the most crucial factor for future success.[12] And, in another survey of more than a thousand CEOs discussed earlier, many cited curiosity and open-mindedness as closely related leadership traits that are becoming increasingly critical in challenging times.[13] These findings raise the question, *Why now?* What is it about the twenty-first-century business landscape that makes creativity and all of the other WHAT IF Skills so invaluable? I suggest it's many of the same factors that have pushed us away from IQ and toward QI. In a Google generation where the facts are at our fingertips, we need to put these facts to work in new and clever ways. It's no longer about information, memorization, and execution. It's about imagination, creativity, and innovation. WHAT IF is the path that takes us there.

It's a Small World

FROM MY SOMEWHAT UNIQUE VANTAGE point of seeing things through both the lens of the rapidly changing business environment and the lens of a pediatrician concerned with how best to help our children become successful, thriving, ready-for-life adults, I see the intersection between the business and parenting worlds almost everywhere I look. Similar to how *The Start-Up of You* and *Business Plans For Dummies* read like parenting books to me the first time I came across them, an e-mail recently landed in my inbox that translated in much the same way. The sender happened to be Disney. Though I can think of no better company where business, creativity, and childhood seamlessly intersect to "make dreams come true," the topic of the message wasn't one that intentionally addressed parenting or children.

Instead, it was from the Disney *Institute*, which holds seminars, workshops, and presentations for business leaders from around the world. The e-mail promoted the Institute's Annual 1-Day Training for businesses and organizations.[14] Some of the action items to be covered in the training included how to

- Tap into your workforce's personal creativity . . .
- Foster an environment that generates ideas . . .
- Develop a collaborative culture
- Encourage risk taking . . .
- Improve business results through structural systems that bring innovation to life

For most, these contemporary business objectives seem straightforward enough. In my eyes, however, this training from Disney, the self-described "Master of Business Solutions and Customer Service," might as well have been promoting a QI Skill parenting course. Swap out the word "workforce" for the word "children" and you've got *parents* learning how to help their *children* turn challenges into greatness and cultivate creativity to its fullest potential. And how might parents do this? Well, a loose translation of the course's offerings might read something like this:

- Tap into your *child's* creativity
- Foster an environment that generates ideas
- Develop WE Skills
- Encourage WOBBLE-ing
- Set your *child* on a path to success through intentional *parenting* that brings your child's WHAT IF Skills to life

In short, the Institute's formula applies as much to parents as it does to businesses. The fact is, the business world is homing in on cultivating the same skills as are those of us who live in the realm of early childhood—we share many of the same goals, challenges, and ideals. In fact, when I look at what's going on in high-level businesses today, I see that what is being done to foster innovation among employees is what my colleagues and I in the pediatric, parenting, and preschool realms do—and have been doing for years—to promote and support creativity and imagination.

When we strip away words that identify *businesses* and *parents*, *employees* and *children*, the differences become barely discernible. As parents, we do it much earlier. And, in reality, if we play our parenting cards right with cultivating WHAT IF and all of the other QI Skills, we'll ultimately decrease the need for programs like Disney's. Our children will enter school, adulthood, and the workplace already equipped with the skills they need and that come naturally to them. We just need to know how to grow them.

Planting the Seeds of Innovation

IF CREATIVITY AND THE ABILITY to ask and act on the question "What if?" are what make us human, then it stands to reason that creativity isn't necessarily something we need to teach young children but rather cultivate and protect. Indeed, Peter Diamandis, whom *Fortune* magazine recently deemed one of the World's Fifty Greatest Leaders,[15] has said, "Entrepreneurs and visionaries imagine the world (and the future) they want to live in, and then they create it. Kids happen to be some of the most imaginative humans around . . . it is critical that they know how important and liberating imagination can be."[16]

Unfortunately, it's all too easy to squelch our children's innate curiosity and creativity rather than liberate them. Psychologists even have a term—enculturation—that explains the notable and unintentional decline in creativity. *Enculturation* refers to how, over time, we adhere to our cultural status quo and fall into routines that make life easier and simpler but that cause us to be less imaginative in our personal and professional realms. We then pass this mentality on to our kids, enculturating them from the time they're born. It's perfectly understandable how this happens.

It's not that we want them to be less creative or less inquisitive; it's simply that we want them to be realistic, learn the rules, and master existing knowledge. Our intentions are good, but the outcomes may not be. When we examine the issue in the context of what we're doing to block our children's developing WHAT IF Skills, it seems we have some parental rethinking to do.

An important shift we can make is to commit to creating a culture that better embraces creativity. We can start by distinguishing between situations that warrant direct answers, instructions, or knowledge sharing and those that are opportunities to encourage our children to practice asking WHAT IF. To this end, I'm often reminded of a trip I took with my children to the Joslyn Art Museum in Omaha when my older son was five years old. We stood in front of a very large and colorful abstract glass sculpture, and he asked me, "What's that?" I nearly replied instinctively with an answer along the lines of, "It's a glass sculpture by a very famous artist named Dale Chihuly that kind of looks like colorful coral under the sea." But then I caught myself and replied, "What do you think it is?"

As parents, we are accustomed to giving answers and we have become quite good at it. But by not settling for the first answer that comes to mind, we can instead set our children's imaginations free. We can hand them the opportunity to discover that there's not always one right answer to everything, that adults aren't all-knowing, and that there's often room for imagination, interpretation, and the question "What if? . . ."

The path that led a young Bart Conner to gymnastics serves as another example of what recognizing and supporting creativity in children can look like—and what is possible when you take a child's natural talents, sense of imagination, and willingness to take a path less traveled and help them fully develop. Conner was also a featured speaker at the 2015 World Creativity Forum, where the Olympic gold medalist shared his story. Long before he ever hung from rings or spun on parallel bars, Conner used to walk down the halls of his elementary school on his hands. Despite the fact that this nontraditional stunt could easily have led him to the principal's office, his parents and principal never said, "Don't walk on your hands. It doesn't lead anywhere." Instead, they directed him to a coach who recognized his unique potential, and the rest became gymnastics history.[17]

The Growth of Creativity

ALTHOUGH CREATIVITY IS NOT YET as easily measured as IQ, fortunately we are finding new and interesting ways—including through brain imaging—to get a clearer picture of just when, where, and how creativity develops in the toddler brain. With the help of books and brain scans, researchers in Cincinnati, led by pediatrician John Hutton, recently took a closer look at the inner workings of imagination. What Dr. Hutton and colleagues' research reinforces is that reading books to young children literally helps build up the part of the brain responsible for seeing things in the "mind's eye." Specifically, they found that preschoolers whose parents reported reading books to them at home showed significantly greater activation of the part of the brain involved in creating mental images.[18] When you think about what this really means, brain research is reinforcing the understanding that reading aloud to young children not only plants the seeds of creativity but also allows us to see—not just in their outward manifestations but also on actual brain scans— the roots of children's imagination taking hold.

And, in case there's any question whether make-believe play influences kids when they go off into the real world, additional research shows that playing pretend enhances a child's capacity for creativity down the road. Researchers have extensively studied the role of pretend play in child development and have found that early imaginative play is associated with increased creative performance years later. In addition, research on notably creative individuals, including Nobel Prize winners and MacArthur Foundation "genius" grant awardees, indicates that these highly accomplished individuals were more likely to have played make-believe and other imaginative games when they were young than others in their fields.[19]

Make-Believe Milestones

UNLIKE THE MORE PREDICTABLE COURSE of early childhood language development that serves to build WE Skills or the motor milestones of WIGGLE, WHAT IF isn't as clearly defined by an outwardly apparent progression of developmental milestones. When you know how to look for the building blocks of WHAT IF, however, you can see in very young babies, sometimes as early as four months old, the first signs of this QI Skill. And these, in time, build toward many other crucial WHAT IF Skills, including make-believe play, belief in superheroes and imaginary friends, and the ability to tell made-up stories. Here's what you can expect to see when it comes to your child's WHAT IF developmental milestones:

- **Six months:** Sometime between four and seven months of age, infants begin to develop the concept of object permanence, the understanding that objects and people still exist even when they can't be seen, heard, touched, smelled, or sensed physically. This intriguing ability allows them to search for a toy hidden under a blanket and find an object placed out of sight.
- **Nine months:** Peek-a-boo is a classic nine-month milestone that takes object permanence to the next level. Babies demonstrate

clearer awareness that people, objects, and even themselves are still there even when they can't be seen.

- **Twelve months:** Children explore toys and objects in lots of new ways beyond just shaking, banging, and throwing, and in ways other than just how they're "supposed" to be used.

- **Eighteen months:** Early forms of creative play start to show up, including the ability to play pretend.

- **Two years:** Children find objects even when they are out of sight under two or three covers, and they now play simple make-believe games. They increasingly start to show interest in interactive play, and imaginative play becomes more elaborate.

- **Three years:** Preschoolers engage in role-play and fantasy play and may frequently switch back and forth between their imaginary worlds and reality. It's not uncommon for three-year-olds to have imaginary friends. Whereas the appearance of imaginary friends used to be the cause of potential concern, it's now recognized to be a very normal and creative aspect in the social-emotional development of preschoolers and older children.

- **Four years:** Four-year-olds enjoy exploring and doing new things in new ways rather than just sticking to the tried and true, and they become even more creative with make-believe play. At this stage, role playing and playing pretend are considered so developmentally important that it actually warrants a visit to the pediatrician for evaluation if a child doesn't show interest in these forms of play. Children this age should also be able to tell you what they think is going to happen next in a book, which indicates a move further into the realm of thinking about, anticipating, and predicting the future (literally asking "Why?" followed by "What if? . . .") rather than just operating within what's already known.

- **Five years:** Kindergarteners become better at distinguishing between what's real and what's imaginary. The goal going forward should be to value both perspectives rather than discounting the world of make-believe.

Making WHAT IF a Reality

BY APPLYING WHAT WE KNOW about creativity, innovation, imagination, and out-of-the-box thinking, it becomes much easier to identify what we, as parents, can do to foster our children's WHAT IF Skills. Research reassures us that our children's creativity is innate and that WHAT IF Skills start developing very early and can be purposefully cultivated. First and foremost, we know that WHAT IF represents the culmination of all the rest of the QI Skills discussed in the preceding chapters. So, to set the foundation for WHAT IF, we need to make sure we focus on ME, WE, WHY, WILL, WIGGLE, and WOBBLE.

And, like many of the other QI Skills, the beauty of WHAT IF is that young children naturally live in a WHAT IF world. Given a supportive environment, they learn to explore, question, and play in ways that strengthen the foundations of this crucial skill. In many ways, our job is made easier by simply creating the time, space, and opportunities children need to frequently flex their WHAT IF muscles. The following is a list of strategies you can apply to doing just that.

Read all about it. Enjoy shared reading time as much, as early, and as often as you can. Reading remains one of the most powerful tools for cultivating WHAT IF (and all of the other QI Skills) for countless reasons, not the least of which includes fostering your child's ability to imagine things that don't actually exist. Some highly creative authors such as Peter Reynolds (in his Creatrilogy consisting of Dot, Ish, and Sky Color[20]) capture the essence of WHAT IF particularly well.

Seek out open-ended toys. Fostering outside-the-box thinking is difficult to do when so many of the toys and games sold today are one-trick ponies meant to be used in ways predetermined by the manufacturer, leaving little to nothing up to your child's imagination. Instead, look for toys that can be used in more creative ways and that promote problem solving and imagination. Some examples of fun, open-ended toys include blocks, playdough, dress-up clothes and props, kitchen sets, and art supplies. Don't forget that everyday objects also offer young children the opportunity to discover new and interesting ways to play. We all know how much they love playing with a cardboard box just as much as what comes inside of it. Beyond the box, infants, toddlers, and preschoolers alike can be endlessly entertained with such open-ended toys as plastic food storage containers, water bottles (without the cap, for safety purposes), and kid-friendly cooking utensils such as spoons and rubber-tipped spatulas (of course, always be sure to use good judgment and supervise for safety).

Toy with their toys. When it comes to WHAT IF–enhancing toys, it helps to think in terms of quality over quantity because a sheer overabundance of toys can stifle kids' creativity. Though the number of children in the United States adds up to only around 3 percent of the world's total, they have been estimated to own approximately 40 percent of the world's toys.[21] To counter this toy-heavy trend, consider a little intentional scarcity. Instead of simply filling your child's toy box with as many bells and whistles as possible, try rotating toys so your child has the chance to focus on and play with only a few at a time. Also make it a habit to pare down a burgeoning toy collection by regularly cleaning out and donating toys (with your child's help).

Praise ideas. Whether they're goofy or genius, show your child that you value her ideas. Try to create an environment for your child in which thinking up and sharing new ideas is encouraged, no matter how silly or outlandish they might seem. And, when possible, entertain children's ideas—help them describe, draw, or even design and build the objects they imagine using household items or supplies, and ask them to elaborate on how they would go about carrying out one of their endearing ideas.

Play along. If your child is playing pretend games or telling made-up stories, encourage this activity by asking her to elaborate. For example, suggest an idea about a pretend scenario or make-believe role that you know will appeal to her or that is relevant to what's going on in her life right now. Then, stand back and watch her imagination flow. If she asks you to play a part, have fun joining in, but remember to keep your role fairly minimal. Provide just enough engagement, suggestions, or props to move her fantasy forward, but allow her to run the show.

Ask thought-provoking questions. Make it a point to start asking and encouraging plenty of open-ended questions to give kids' minds the freedom to devise creative and contemplative answers. Although questions with definitive answers are important for helping young children build their knowledge base ("What color is the grass?" "What does the dog say?"), as your child's imagination, vocabulary, and WHAT IF Skills blossom be sure to ask a growing number of open-ended, WHAT IF, and thought-provoking questions such as "What did you think of? . . ." "What do you think would happen if? . . ." and "Why do you think? . . ."

Tell stories. Model making up fanciful stories to encourage your child's imagination. If this isn't exactly second nature for you, start by selecting a topic that you know piques your child's interest. For my son who loved elephants, I might talk about a recent trip to the zoo, for example, but then use what he knew and had actually experienced as a starting point for something to happen next that was fanciful, made up, unlikely, or silly. When my kids were younger, it was up to me to keep the imaginative storyline going. But as they got older, about four or five years old, and with practice, they started to take over and run with the story themselves while I simply played along and made it a point to ask lots of questions that kept the stories charging forward even longer. This was a simple but very telling display of what imaginative ideas children can come up with when you commit to unleashing their creative potential.

Unplug. A certain amount of exposure to developmentally appropriate electronic toys and digital technologies can be useful. Too much, however, has the potential to take away your child's motivation to ask WHAT IF since open-ended play, boredom, and meandering have become all too infrequent occurrences in today's electronic universe. Many electronic toys are prescriptive: they require certain behaviors or actions to function instead of allowing your child's imagination to run the show. In fact, a 2015 study found that parents and children interact with electronic toys much differently from how they do with traditional toys like blocks and books. Babies vocalize less, parents speak fewer words, and the nature of the interaction is significantly different. Parents are more likely to give behavioral-related cues such as "do this" or "press that" than ask WHAT IF questions relevant to the context.[22] Given that parents are key in cultivating children's creativity and that these toys tend to talk and interact with our children in our place (and often in very limited ways), we run the risk of limiting kids' opportunities for using their WHAT IF Skills the more time we allow them to spend in front of these devices.

Take the path less traveled. Making a change as simple as taking a different route when walking outside, exploring a new-to-you neighborhood, or finding a new nature walk opens up a world of possibilities for you and your children to put WHAT IF into action. Although there's value in maintaining routines (for us and for our children), sometimes we unintentionally develop ruts where there needn't be any—and in so doing limit opportunities to imagine and explore.

Question your rules. Be judicious in insisting that things must always be done in a certain way or that all rules must always be followed. Yes, rule following is an important skill to master. And, yes, legitimate safety concerns (and well-thought-out safety-related rules) should always come first. But, as parents, we also need to consider whether the many rules of early childhood truly serve important purposes. If a child wants to climb up a slide instead of sliding down it (when there's no one else at the top about to come down, of course), for example, or he wants to take apart or try out a new and different way of using a particular toy, don't automatically put your foot down. Renowned developmental neuroscientist Adele Diamond concludes that the ability to disassemble and recombine elements in new ways is the essence of creativity.[23] Instead, consider these sorts of early questioning of the "rules" as representing the exploration and the discovery of different ways to do things and uncommon uses of common objects that all but define innovation.

Color outside the lines. Doing arts and crafts is a wonderful and very natural way for children to explore their imagination and creativity. Whereas learning to color inside the lines serves many useful purposes (including developing fine motor skills and helping kids learn how to listen and follow directions), be sure to give them just as much time to color outside the lines and even create their own lines. Provide young children with age-appropriate art supplies and just enough instruction and supervision, but remember to allow them to create something that doesn't already exist in someone else's mind's eye. In this regard, I am reminded of the daily creative art activities we offered at the childcare center I used to run. I often needed to gently remind the teachers that I'd rather walk by a board displaying toddler and preschool art projects and *not* have a clear picture of what I was looking at than see a dozen identical bunnies with every cotton ball tail glued perfectly in place. To gain insights into your child's early creative expressions, also remember to have her describe to you what she's made. There's no doubt her answers will surprise and impress you.

Let them be bored. Instead of committing to shuttling preschoolers between one defined activity and the next on a day-to-day basis, remember to factor in plenty of "free" time. The idea runs counter to so much of what today's parenting world has come to believe is necessary for helping children learn—engagement, interaction, and entertainment—but has tremendous value for budding WHAT IF Skills. Allowing young children ample free time enables them to explore what they've learned and engage in WHAT IF ways of thinking. As neuropsychologist and creativity researcher Rex Jung has said, "If you're constantly in knowledge acquisition mode, there's not that quiet time to put it together. . . . You have to have the raw materials in place . . . but you also have to have the time to put them together."[24]

QI for All

Children are the living messages we send to a
time we will not see.

—Neil Postman, *The Disappearance of Early
Childhood*

CONGRATULATIONS! EMPOWERED WITH NEW PARENTING
insights and the ability to see your parenting role in its
much bigger world context, you now have what it takes to
apply all of today's business-savvy, data-driven, and technology-
fueled know-how, as well as all that the Information Age has put
right at your fingertips, to more purposefully raise your child
to succeed in a rapidly changing world. Although the strategies
you'll use to get there involve many seemingly small, everyday
steps, the cumulative results will represent no minor parenting
feat. I hope you have a very clear sense of parenting purpose and
feel a sense of parental pride in knowing just how valuable your
earliest brain-building and QI Skill–cultivating efforts will be
for your child's future.

In recognizing how important caring, responsive adults
and nurturing social interactions are beginning early in life, I
also hope that you will take a moment to consider (if you aren't
already convinced) just how critical this sort of supportive

foundation is for all children. In a world where QI Skills are living up to their name as key and powerful life forces and proving to be invaluable in improving quality of life for those who possess them, the fact is it's becoming increasingly difficult to succeed without them. Rather than succumbing to the competitive parenting mindset of simply wanting to give our own children the best, my hope is that we feel empowered to make sure all children have the benefit of nurturing social interactions early in life that will lay the groundwork for their lifelong success as well. When it comes to achieving QI Skills for all, however, we still have a ways to go.

A World Full of Gaps

AS GLOBALLY CONNECTED AS THE world may be, it is also a world full of gaps. Gaps that span from the boardroom to the playroom, from innovation, skills, and technology gaps to opportunity, education, and even word gaps. If addressing these disparities seems like far too mighty a task for busy parents of young children to take on all by ourselves, that's because it is.

Fortunately, the daunting task of how best to address these disparities doesn't fall solely on our shoulders. Entire books, organizations, and even political campaigns are now focused on addressing these pressing concerns. That's not to say, however, that we don't have a critical role to play in this effort. In fact, it is *because* we are parents that we are optimally suited to understand just how important it is to advocate for what every child needs.

As we dedicate ourselves to making the strategic connections that will change our own children's lives, making their world a better place should also include our collective commitment to helping close these gaps so that all children can live, learn, and thrive.

> **Facing the Facts**
>
> Simply titled "Still Face Experiment," a short YouTube video posted in 2009 and narrated by the director of Harvard's Child Development Unit, managed, in less than three minutes, to help its more than four million viewers get a feel for just how impactful the day-to-day interactions of caring, responsive parents—or the lack thereof—can be on the well-being of children. Watch it and you'll likely be unable to look away or look past the fact that every young child needs and deserves a caring, responsive adult in their daily lives.[1]

At a Loss for Words

THE WORD GAP IS AS good a place as any to start. We now know a toddler's vocabulary can say a whole lot about how likely he or she is to fare in school, work, and even in life. The message is clear: there's more riding on children's earliest interactions and language development than many people realize.

This powerful message also makes results from a landmark study conducted by two University of Kansas child psychologists, Betty Hart and Todd Risley, all the more compelling. Hart and Risley studied the amount of spoken language very young children were exposed to in their homes and discovered that it was closely correlated with a family's socioeconomic status. They found that children in low-income families heard about 600 words per hour compared with the more than 2,100 words per hour children of professional parents heard.[2] On a day-to-day basis, that's a sizable gap. But by age three, it adds up to a staggering 30 million fewer words. What's more, it's not just the quantity but the *quality* of words that typifies this enormous chasm.

Subsequent research at Stanford further reinforces that dramatic differences in vocabulary are evident as early as eighteen months, and by age two, less-advantaged children may already be an average of six months behind their toddler peers.[3]

Considering just how crucial all of the early social, serve-and-return interactions are for strengthening babies' social connections and neural networks, the fact that this poverty-driven word gap exists should leave us all at a loss for words.

> "The best metric of child poverty may have to do not with income but with how often a child is spoken and read to."
>
> —Nicholas Kristof, "Too Small to Fail," *New York Times,* 2016

Building Resilience

WHEN I FIRST PUT ALL the pieces of the early brain and social-emotional development "story" together and learned what I learned about the potential impact they have for young children, I was compelled to share it with everyone I knew. I set out to develop the QI Skills as a way for parents (and anyone else dedicated to the well-being of children) to embrace the lead role we have the honor of playing in this story. We love our babies and we coo, talk, read, play, and sing to them, but what we're doing is so much greater than eliciting smiles, babbles, and even first words. We're parenting with purpose and nurturing the QI

Skills that will help shape our children's future. In a fair and just world, my hope is that we also find (and fund) ways to share with *all* parents our insights regarding these skills and how best to cultivate them.

Director of Harvard's Center on the Developing Child Jack Shonkoff, along with his colleagues, has found that poverty and adversity in early childhood don't just influence children's learning and educational success, they have potentially neurotoxic effects that can compromise children's very ability to learn during the time we know to be most critical for foundational brain growth and development.[4] Although we are still a long way from figuring out how to end the cycle of multigenerational poverty that puts unimaginable and hazardous stresses on young children and their families, what Shonkoff and many others have determined is that caring, responsive adults who help build executive function capacities and instill adaptive skills early in children's lives can serve as effective buffers against the neurotoxic toll that poverty takes on the developing brain and on children's futures.

Pediatricians and neuroscientists are not alone in addressing the implications poverty and adversity have on children's future life potential. Nobel Prize–winning economist James Heckman at the University of Chicago is helping lead this charge, too. In researching the economic impact of investing in the first five years, Heckman concludes that the most effective way to produce social mobility, equal opportunity, and lifetime success is by employing the very same strategies we've discussed throughout this book: making available to young children, from birth to age five, nurturing environments that promote their physical, mental, and social development. As one of the country's leading advocates for investing in young children, Heckman shines light on the fact that nurturing environments are what "empower children with the capabilities to flourish as dignified and engaged citizens and workers throughout their lives."[5] The work of both Shonkoff and Heckman, along with that of many others, suggests that regardless of whether our focus is on individual, societal, or economic returns on investment, investing in children and investing early yield the biggest returns of all.

Making Hope Happen

"Although some people still believe that hope is too 'soft' to study scientifically, other researchers and I have convincing evidence that hopeful thoughts and behavior propel everyone toward well-being and success; that hope underlies purpose-driven action, from showing up for school to leading organizations and communities; that it correlates positively with health and even longevity; and that it does not depend on income level or IQ."

—Shane Lopez, renowned hope researcher, Gallup senior scientist, and author of *Making Hope Happen: Create the Future You Want for Yourself and Others*

Hope Is QI

IT HAS BEEN SAID THAT the difference between optimism and hope is that hope involves not only being able to imagine something better, but feeling like you have the ability to make it so.[6] Building brains and nurturing QI Skills is what will give children the ability to not only imagine a better world than the one they're born in to but also believe they have the ability to make this dream a reality, regardless of the zip code in which they are raised.

By applying what we know about neurons to what we do in our neighborhoods, we can help achieve this vision by looking within our own communities, cities, and states to discover and support efforts that help to ensure all children have access to nurturing environments, caring and responsive adults, and early education resources—factors that help to close gaps early and, in so doing, make a lifelong difference.

From Wild West to Gold Rush

WHEN IT COMES TO SETTING children up for success, the good news is that we know what to do, we know when to do it, and we know how to do it for our own children. The question that remains is: How can we do it for all children? What gives me hope is that what once felt more like the Wild West of early childhood in terms of isolated efforts, overlooked research, and insufficient funding has started to bear more resemblance to a gold rush. Although many pioneers in early childhood have spent decades paving the way for what's now underfoot, they were often going it alone, without the attention, support, and backing of society as a whole.

Spurred on by our new and compelling twenty-first-century understanding of the toddler brain, the path forward is becoming ever clearer. Sectors of our society as far-flung as business, economics, the justice system, and the military are stepping up alongside pediatricians, psychologists, educators, social scientists, and neuroscientists to focus much-needed attention on our children's first five years.

So what exactly has been happening in the world of early childhood that's causing all heads to turn and ears to perk up? The broadening awareness of the very same science that underpins this book is leading more and more people to the inevitable conclusion that what happens in the earliest years, months, and even weeks of life is supremely important.

For anyone who realizes that not all parents know about the surprising science behind their child's development much less possess the parenting skills they need and for all those who recognize that nearly one in four US children are living in poverty and who take the time to connect the dots, the compelling case for investing in these parents and their children's futures is being laid out before us more urgently than ever before. It's not hard to see why the rush is on.

And on it is. Efforts such as Too Small to Fail's Talking Is Teaching,[7] Vroom,[8] Zero to Three,[9] and the 30 Million Words Initiative[10] are but a few of the many efforts committed to providing parents with the information and support they need to give their children the best possible start. National, Fortune 500, and even global business leaders are banding together through an organization called ReadyNation to promote the importance of baby talk and the relevance of early childhood development to workforce development.[11] Economists are looking at human youth capital and validating that early investment stands to pay impressively large dividends.[12] Even the Federal Reserve is joining in, cohosting early childhood discussions around issues of financial support for investment in everything from high-quality pre-K to home visitation, prenatal programs, and more.[13]

The challenge at hand is admittedly complex. As senior Gallup scientist and world-renowned hope researcher Shane Lopez states, the way from the present to the future is seldom a straight line, and almost never a single one.[14] Yet I believe there's still hope. In recognizing that innovative solutions are most likely to be found at the intersection of diverse concepts, disciplines, and industries, I truly believe that, if we continue to come together and pool our collective efforts, research, and resources for the benefit of young children, we can make QI for all a reality.

Getting Down to Business

In his April 2014 testimony before the US Senate Committee on Health, Education, Labor, and Pensions, former Procter & Gamble chairman and CEO John E. Pepper stated:

> In order for American businesses to compete success-fully in a global economy, employees must have the knowledge, skills and abilities to be communicators, collaborators and critical thinkers. Research confirms that the foundation for these social and fundamental education skills is developed during a child's earliest years. The first five years of life are a unique period of brain development, which lays the foundation for lifelong learning. The achievement gap starts to open as early as age two or three, when research shows that low-income children know half as many words as higher-income children. Children also show a significant achievement gap in math by kindergarten entry. . . . In business, we rarely have the luxury of making investment decisions with as much evidence as we have to support the economic value of investing in early childhood development and education.

A Message to Our Children

IN DECEMBER 2015, SHORTLY AFTER the birth of his first child, Facebook founder Mark Zuckerberg posted for all the world to see a touching letter he'd written to his newborn daughter.[15] It began,

Dear Max,
Your mother and I don't yet have the words to describe the hope you give us for the future. Your new life is full of promise, and we hope you will be happy and healthy so you can explore it fully. You've already given us a reason to reflect on the world we hope you live in.

In clear and thoughtful parenting prose, he continued:

Like all parents, we want you to grow up in a world better than ours today. . . . We will do our part to make this happen, not only because we love you, but also because we have a moral responsibility to all children in the next generation.

Whereas the financial contribution that Zuckerberg and his wife, Priscilla Chan, pledged to improve the world for their daughter's generation and many generations to follow was truly astounding in both its size and scope, the accompanying pledge they made as parents—to value *all* children and act on the belief that *every* child should have access to opportunities regardless of the circumstances into which they are born—is a pledge that each and every one of us can afford to make. As a society, it's one we can't afford not to.

Appendix 1

QI Resources:
Reading All About It—
A QI Collection for Kids

A sampling of children's books that can help cultivate QI

AS WE'VE DISCUSSED, INTRODUCING YOUNG children to books is one of the very best ways to engage them with stories, emotions, and experiences that will help them understand the world they live in and expand their worldview. Reading aloud with your child is about far more than just the book itself, the literal sharing of words on a page, or helping your child learn to read. It is also about cultivating a shared love of reading and represents what we now know is at the very heart of nurturing the seven QI Skills that will help your child succeed in life: a shared, meaningful interaction that you can enjoy with your child every day.

As you start out, look for books that are tailored to your child's age and stage of development, such as books your baby can touch, feel, and even drool on. This helps introduce reading as an activity you can share from the day you enter parenthood. As your child grows, simply add books that introduce new sights, sounds, emotions, entertaining rhymes, and child-relevant challenges to your growing collection.

Although there are countless wonderful children's books from which to choose, certain books focus on illustrating the QI Skills more specifically and certain books have QI Skills written all over them. You'll also find that individual books often draw on multiple QI Skills, while WHY is a skill that is captured not so much in the words of any one book but in your child's inquisitiveness and interest in all books.

From personal and friend- and colleague-recommended favorites to classic and contemporary books alike, the following is just a sampling of what you can find when you start exploring the world of children's books with QI Skills in mind.

ME and WE

- *Baby Faces Board Book* by DK Publishing. Both ME and WE Skills depend on the ability to recognize, understand, and name emotions, which makes this "delightful book full of fun faces just right for babies" an enjoyable (and durable) way to introduce very young children to such important emotions as happy, sad, puzzled, angry, worried, and several more.

- *Duck & Goose: Goose Needs a Hug* by Tad Hills. This simple tale, in a literal sense, is about a sad goose whose feathered friends recognize that he is feeling sad and try to figure out just what it will take to make him happy again. In a broader sense, however, it's about the relationships, ability to read emotions, and ability to express empathy that are at the heart of WE.

- *The Grouchy Ladybug* by Eric Carle. Feeling grouchy is not an uncommon emotion for toddlers, teens, and even adults. Fortunately, those who share this story with young children can help them not only recognize this emotion but also learn from Eric Carle's ill-tempered ladybug the ME and WE Skills necessary to control the socially unacceptable impulses that tend to accompany it. In the grouchy ladybug's case, this includes screaming, shouting, refusing to share, and just generally not getting along.

- *I Say, You Say Feelings!* by Tad Carpenter. As one of a series of lift-the-flap books, this one in particular focuses on the world of emotions and offers both illustrations and under-the-flap descriptions to help children explore and hone their understanding of emotions.

- *It's Mine* and *Little Blue and Little Yellow* by Leo Lionni. Two endearing books that capture the power, importance, and challenge of learning WE Skills. The former focuses on impulse control and learning to share, while the latter provides a colorful and simple (albeit somewhat abstract) view of friendship, differences, and tolerance.

- Elizabeth Verdick's series of highly practical impulse- and self-control books that include *Teeth Are Not for Biting, Feet Are Not for Kicking, Voices Are Not for Yelling,* and *Words Are Not for Hurting,* as well as Martine Agassi's *Hands Are Not for Hitting* and Verdick's related *Calm Down Time* and *Listening Time*

- Cornelia Maude Spelman's *When I Feel . . .* series that includes books addressing a range of emotions such as *Worried, Angry, Sad, Scared,* and *Jealous*

- *Time Out for Sophie, Sophie's Terrible Twos, Hands Off, Harry!,* and *Yoko's World of Kindness* by Rosemary Wells

- *All for Me and None for All; Me, First*; and *Listen, Buddy* by Helen Lester

- *The Way I Feel* by Janan Cain

- *The Way I Act* by Steve Metzger

- *I Can Do It Too!* by Karen Baicker

- *Go! Go! Go! Stop!* by Charise Mericle Harper

- *A Color of His Own* by Leo Lionni

- *Amazing Me: It's Busy Being 3!* by Julia Cook and Laura Jana
- *The Feelings Book* by Todd Parr
- *Hurty Feelings* by Helen Lester
- *My Many Colored Days* by Dr. Seuss
- *How are You Peeling? Foods With Moods* by Saxton Freymann and Joost Elffers. This book offers a particularly appealing and unique way to engage readers young and old alike, providing a literal representation of various emotions while also serving as a model of creativity by putting produce to novel use.
- *When Sophie Gets Angry—Really, Really Angry* and *When Sophie's Feelings Are Really, Really Hurt* by Molly Bang
- *Happy Hippo, Angry Duck: A Book of Moods* by Sandra Boynton
- *The Big Book of Hugs* by Nick Ortner
- *A Great Big Cuddle: Poems for the Very Young* by Michael Rosen
- *My Heart Is Like a Zoo* by Michael Hall
- *Mine!* by Sue Heap
- *Little Blue Truck* by Alice Schertle
- *How Full Is Your Bucket? For Kids* by Tom Rath
- Anthony Lewis's baby sign language series, *Sign About* series, including *Getting Ready, Play Time, Meal Time,* and *Going Out*
- *Baby Signs: A Baby-Sized Introduction to Speaking with Sign Language* illustrated by Joy Allen

WIGGLE (Books Children Can Wiggle To)

WHAT ALL THESE BOOKS HAVE in common is that they lend themselves to being actively enjoyed in a very physical sense. Whether encouraging your child to clap, point to body parts, reach out to touch and feel, or jump along, each is well suited to foster children's early love of reading while also recognizing that sometimes they just can't help but WIGGLE.

- *From Head to Toe* by Eric Carle
- *Ten Tiny Toes* by Caroline Jayne Church
- *Pat-a-Cake* and *We All Fall Down* by Mary Brigid Barrett
- *Jump, Frog, Jump!* by Robert Kalan
- *Wheels on the Bus* and *Shake My Sillies Out* by Raffi
- *Sign and Sing Along: Itsy-Bitsy Spider, Head Shoulders Knees and Toes, If You're Happy and You Know It,* and *His Little Piggy* by Annie Kubler
- *Where Is Baby's Belly Button?* by Karen Katz
- *Baby Touch and Feel: Baby Animals*
- *The Itsy-Bitsy Spider* by Rosemary Wells
- DK Touch and Feel series, including *Colors and Shapes, Animals, Baby Animals, Cuddly Animals, Bedtime, Bathtime, Mealtime, Farm, Noisy Farm, First Words, Numbers, Playtime, Splish! Splash!, Puppies and Kittens, Trucks, Wild Animals,* and *Things That Go*

WHY, WILL, WOBBLE and WHAT IF

- Creatrilogy boxed set that includes Ish, Dot, and Sky Color by Peter Reynolds. Right down to this trilogy's creative title, author Peter Reynolds makes it clear that he believes in the value of seeing the world differently, starting small, and the power of WHAT IF. Ish and The Dot have for years ranked high on my list of personal favorite books that illustrate how to cultivate children's creative spirit. With Sky Color's message about looking beyond the expected, this third book in the trilogy is deserving of its spot alongside the others.
- *Beautiful Oops!* by Barney Saltzberg. What do you get from a book that proposes turning an accidental tear in a paper into the roaring mouth of an alligator, or taking a spill on a drawing and turning it into the shape of a goofy animal? A whimsically

engaging book about WOBBLE meant to leave parents and children alike with the notion that "a mistake is an adventure in creativity" and "a portal of discovery."

- *The Little Engine That Could* by Watty Piper. This children's book classic has WILL written all over it, from its very first "I think I can." An iconic Little Blue Engine determinedly commits to the daunting task of trying to get a broken-down train filled with toys and treats to the children waiting on the other side of the mountain. With millions of copies in print, *The Little Engine That Could* has met with tremendous success, not only in reaching the top of the mountain but in helping children and parents alike embrace and believe in the power of WILL.

- *A Perfectly Messed-Up Story* by Patrick McDonnell. The use of both "perfectly" and "messed-up" in the title should serve as a giveaway that this book—in characteristic McDonnell form—is about WIGGLE-ability and overcoming whatever obstacles may come along (which in Little Louie's case come in the form of a blob of jelly or chunky peanut butter) rather than persistently pursuing perfection.

- *What Do You Do with an Idea?* by Kobi Yamada. On the surface, this is a story of one brilliant idea and the child who helps to bring it into the world. In recognizing that children's ideas need just as much cultivation in a nurturing environment as children themselves do to spread their wings and take flight, however, Yamada, starting in monotone but gradually introducing color, paints a picture of children's budding WHY and WHAT IF Skills and how they stand to change the world.

- *Beautiful Hands* by Bret Baumgarten. Said to be inspired by the author's daily question to his young daughter, "What will your beautiful hands do today?" this inspiring book reinforces for children and parents the fundamental belief in a world full of endless possibilities that can be achieved through the power of WHAT IF.

- *Harold and the Purple Crayon* by Crockett Johnson
- *Art* by Patrick McDonnell
- *Perfect Square* by Michael Hall
- *Horton Hatches the Egg* by Dr. Seuss
- *The Most Magnificent Thing* by Ashley Spires
- *Peep Leap* by Elizabeth Verdick
- *The Artist Who Painted a Blue Horse* by Eric Carle

The Purpose of Parenting and Unconditional Love

- *My Shining Star* and *Hand in Hand* by Rosemary Wells. Best-selling author (and good friend) Rosemary Wells gets right to the heart of what it means, as well as what it looks like on a day-to-day basis, to be a caring, responsive parent.
- *You Are My I Love You* by Maryann Cusimano Love. Composed of simple rhymes and lighthearted imagery, this book is but one of many that touchingly captures the special bond between parent and child.
- *I Love You More* by Laura Duksta
- *Mama, Do You Love Me?* by Barbara M. Joosse
- *I Love You As Much . . .* by Laura Krauss Melmed
- *The I LOVE YOU Book* by Todd Parr
- *Guess How Much I Love You?* by Sam McBratney
- *Daddy Hugs* by Karen Katz
- *You Are My Sunshine* by Caroline Jayne Church
- *I Love You Through and Through* by Bernadette Rossetti Shustak

Appendix 2

QI Resources:
Putting QI into Parenting Practice

Additional parenting books, organizations, and resources that can help you parent with purpose and cultivate QI

IF YOUR READING TIME IS limited, then by all means focus on the books in the preceding appendix and on enjoying reading books with your child. If, however, you find yourself with some extra time and interest, here is a sampling of related parenting books and evidence-based resources that align well with the concepts I've presented in *The Toddler Brain*.

Parenting Books

- *Heading Home with Your Newborn: From Birth to Reality* by pediatricians Laura A. Jana and Jennifer Shu (American Academy of Pediatrics, 3rd ed., 2015). This, of course, is the book I coauthored in order to offer parents a strong foundation of both nuts-and-bolts insights and provide a reassuring support structure for practical, positive parenting.

- *Mind in the Making: The Seven Essential Life Skills Every Child Needs* by the founder of the Families and Work Institute, Ellen Galinsky (HarperCollins, 2010). Here's where you'll definitely want to turn if you love the research and want to know in much greater detail more about the leaders in this field, their intriguing studies, and how best to practically apply the results to your day-to-day, brain-building interactions with your child from day one. No one I know has pulled it all together more comprehensively for parents.

- *The Philosophical Baby: What Children's Minds Tell Us About Truth, Love, and the Meaning of Life* by psychology professor Alison Gopnik (Farrar, Straus and Giroux, 2009). Here's where you can find in-depth discussions about the surprising and sometimes complex science behind your child's development from someone renowned in the field for her hands-on research on the baby brain.

- *How Children Succeed: Grit, Curiosity, and the Hidden Power of Character* by Paul Tough (Houghton Mifflin Harcourt, 2013). The title should be enough to make you curious, and should you pursue your curiosity further, you won't be disappointed. Author Paul Tough does a masterful and highly acclaimed job of summarizing the education landscape—profiling people, programs, and research that are guiding our twenty-first-century insights into how children succeed as well as how they can be potentially led astray on their path to success.

- *Mindset: The New Psychology of Success* by psychology professor Carol Dweck (Ballantine Books, 2008). A book that falls somewhere between parenting and psychology, this one critically defines the difference between a fixed and a growth mindset—key (and QI) concepts that most certainly apply to raising and educating children. Whether you read Dweck's more in-depth description of her influential research or not, the growth mindset is one you'll definitely want to adopt as your own and foster in your children.

- *Building Resilience in Children and Teens* by pediatrician Kenneth R. Ginsburg (American Academy of Pediatrics, 2014). Although Ginsberg, a highly trained adolescent medicine specialist, focuses on older children, the concepts he conveys are very much aligned (not to mention presented in a compelling way) and will give you lots to look forward to as you commit to building your child's QI Skills throughout their childhood and beyond.

- *UnSelfie: Why Empathetic Kids Succeed in Our All-About-Me World* by Michele Borba (Simon & Schuster/Touchstone, 2016). Already familiar with Michele Borba's longstanding and well-respected contributions to the areas of parenting, education, and empathy, a sneak-peek at her new book, *UnSelfie* (not to mention its impressive amount of expert praise) just before its 2016 release, had me enthused about what it offers on the importance of empathy and how to encourage it in our children.

- *All Joy and No Fun: The Paradox of Modern Parenthood* by Jennifer Senior (HarperCollins, 2014). This is but one of many books that will help you consider the alternatives to tiger and helicopter parenting and renew your sense of fun-loving parenting purpose. If you don't have time to read it, you can also tune in to Senior's 2015 TED Talk to get the gist.

QI Organizations and Resources

- **American Academy of Pediatrics (AAP):** As a longstanding member of and spokesperson for the American Academy of Pediatrics, I would be remiss if I didn't start the list by directing attention to the wealth of valuable and trustworthy sites and sources the AAP is dedicated to making available to parents.

From early brain and child development and early literacy-specific information to the all-encompassing healthychildren .org website, this should be considered one of your most trusted parenting sources.

- **Zero to Three:** With a clearly defined (and clearly critical) age focus, Zero to Three's mission is to ensure that all babies and toddlers have a strong start in life. Founded more than thirty-five years ago by leading researchers and clinicians, this is an organization that parents and professionals alike turn to and trust. It boasts a very easy-to-navigate website that is full of practical, highly relevant, easy-to-read insights for new parents. Just head to www.zerotothree.org and click on "Explore Our Topics" for everything from early development and well-being to early learning, early intervention, and more.

- **National Association for the Education of Young Children (NAEYC):** Although technically a professional membership organization for early childhood professionals (numbering over sixty thousand), NAEYC's commitment to promoting high-quality early learning for all young children by connecting early childhood policy and research to everyday practice makes it an organization with lots of useful resources, and one that's well worth parents knowing about. Visit www.naeyc.org.

- **Centers for Disease Control and Prevention (CDC):** In relation to fostering QI Skills, the CDC is one of the most highly trusted sources for information on the developmental milestones of early childhood. Simply Googling "Learn the Signs" will get you to the CDC's top-ranked webpage that lists the common motor, social-emotional, and cognitive milestones of early childhood broken down by age from two months to five years (also found more directly by following the link www.cdc.gov/ncbddd /actearly/milestones).

- **Reach Out and Read (ROR):** Officially described as one of the country's most well-recognized and longstanding early literacy nonprofit organizations, ROR makes use of a very strong and ever-expanding evidence base of early literacy research to support its pediatrician-led efforts to provide all children with the books, parental support, and skills they need to develop critical early reading skills beginning in infancy. Be sure to check out the compilation of milestones of early literacy development (www.reachoutandread.org/resource-center/literacy-materials /literacy-milestones/). Given that reading books to babies and young children can play an instrumental role in all aspects of QI Skill development, you're likely to find them motivating, instructive, and invaluable.

- **The Center on the Developing Child:** This is admittedly not somewhere to go for light bedtime or beach reading. But it is a definite go-to for anyone searching for supporting briefs, summaries of studies, short videos, and more that collectively serve to pull together essentially all that we know and that is being discovered about early brain and child development. With briefs on such topics as the foundations of lifelong health, the science of early childhood development, and building the brain's "air traffic control" system, the Center on the Developing Child, under the direction of Dr. Jack Shonkoff, is leading the way for the benefit of all future generations as it reaches for breakthroughs using science-based innovation. Visit www.developing child.harvard.edu.

Appendix 3

QI Resources:
QI Business, Leadership, Innovation, and Psychology Books

Some surprisingly parenting-relevant books about real-world QI from outside the parenting world

- *The Start-Up of You: Adapt to the Future, Invest in Yourself, and Transform Your Career* by LinkedIn cofounder Reid Hoffman and Ben Casnocha (Crown Business, 2012). This is the book—complete with insights into today's world of business, innovation, and start-ups—that convinced me that the assembly of a twenty-first-century toolkit of skills was a vision that extended well beyond the parenting world and that there should be a "Start-Up of Your Baby" equivalent (which over time became *The Toddler Brain*).

- *The Medici Effect: What Elephants and Epidemics Can Teach Us About Innovation* by Frans Johansson (Harvard Business School Press, 2006). If you want to further explore the concept of innovation occurring at the intersection of diverse groups of people, professions, and organizations, this is one of the books that first headed me down that path.

- *Business Plans Kit For Dummies* by Steven Peterson, Peter Jaret, and Barbara Schenck (Wiley Publishing, 2010). Okay, you don't really have to read this one unless you have a whole lot of extra time on your hands (or simply can't sleep). But if, for some reason, you decide to—try crossing out the words "business" and "employer" and replacing them with the word "parent." Make the same switch with "employee" and "child" and you might be surprised, amused, and entertained by the unexpected relevance when it comes to more strategically ensuring our parenting hopes and dreams come to fruition.

- *Wellbeing: The Five Essential Elements* by Tom Rath and Jim Harter (Gallup Press, 2010) and *Making Hope Happen: Create the Future You Want for Yourself and Others* by Shane J. Lopez (Simon & Schuster, 2013). These books will make you think (not to mention convince you with lots of interesting research) about just what it is that defines well-being and hope, concepts you can apply to both yourself and to what you ultimately want for your child.

- *Start with Why: How Great Leaders Inspire Everyone to Take Action* (Penguin, 2009) and *Leaders Eat Last: Why Some Teams Pull Together and Others Don't* (Penguin, 2014) both by Simon Sinek. Interesting and fairly profound books. All it will take to make the connection to parenting is to read them while intentionally thinking about the role you stand to play as a parent and how best to rise to the challenge.

- *Drive: The Surprising Truth About What Motivates Us* by New York Times best-selling author Daniel H. Pink (Riverhead Books, 2011). Here's your one-stop shop for everything to do with the science of will, motivation, and drive. Somewhat research-dense in places, but all valuable, relevant, and deserving of its NYT best-seller status.

- *Abundance: The Future Is Better Than You Think* by futurist Peter Diamandis and Steven Kotler (Simon & Schuster/Free Press, 2012). Offering a leading-edge worldview of the world your children are likely to live in. Very big, yet focused on innovation, technology, and exponential change, this is a book for those who like new, large ideas with interesting stories, examples, and innovations to back them up.

- *Work Rules! Insights from Inside Google That Will Transform How You Live and Lead* by Google's head of People Operations Laszlo Bock (Hachette Book Group, 2015). Given that Google is, by its very nature, a company that deals in data, the introspective approach Bock takes to look at common workforce issues and practices, consider human nature, and identify the skills proving most valuable in today's world of work can prove intriguing.

- *The Innovator's DNA: Mastering the Five Skills of Disruptive Innovators* by Jeff Dyer, Hal Gregersen, and Clayton Christensen (Harvard Business Review Press, 2011). Harvard Business School professor Clayton Christensen and colleagues are no strangers to the science of innovation. Skills overlap, concepts are applicable, and the research behind them (both Christensen's and all of the rest cited throughout the book) is interesting.

Organizations and Resources

- **ReadyNation:** This nonprofit business membership organization is a part of the Council for a Strong America, which unites five organizations of different types of powerful leaders preparing the next generation to be well educated, physically fit, and prepared for productive lives. Since 2006, ReadyNation has been leveraging the experience, influence, and expertise of more than fifteen hundred business executives to promote public policies and programs that build a stronger workforce and economy. These "unexpected" voices have made a bottom-line case for effective, bipartisan investments in children, from birth to young adulthood, as the future workforce that will drive success in the global marketplace. I belong to and actively support this group, whose members range from current and former Fortune 500 CEOs to small business owners and midlevel executives. ReadyNation is an ideal resource for those who want to know more about the economic and business case for investing early, including what can and is being done at the company, community, and policy levels. You can find more information at www.strongnation.org/readynation.

- **The Heckman Equation:** Although this is the brainchild of University of Chicago's Nobel Prize–winning economist James Heckman, don't let that intimidate you. What Heckman and colleagues masterfully do, with support from the Pritzker Children's Initiative, is brilliantly weave together the science of early brain and child development with the economic evidence for why it is so critical for our children's (and our country's) future. Information is scientific and well supported but also made more easily accessible and understandable for "anyone looking to offer upstream solutions to the biggest problems facing America." Visit www.heckmanequation.org.

Notes

Introduction:
The Start-Up of Your Baby

1. Reid Hoffman and Ben Casnocha, *The Start-Up of You: Adapt to the Future, Invest in Yourself, and Transform Your Career* (New York: Crown Business, 2012).

2. Steve Denning, "What the Emerging Creative Economy Means for Jobs" (presentation, Innovation 4 Jobs [i4j] Summit, Stanford Research Institute [SRI], Palo Alto, CA, January 28, 2016).

3. "About the Medici Group," Medici Group Consulting, accessed August 13, 2016.

4. Frans Johansson, *The Medici Effect: What Elephants and Epidemics Can Teach Us About Innovation* (Boston: Harvard Business School Press, 2006).

5. Hoffman and Casnocha, *Start-Up of You*, 224.

6. Jennifer Senior, *All Joy and No Fun: The Paradox of Modern Parenthood* (New York: HarperCollins, 2014), 10.

7. Steven Peterson, Peter Jaret, and Barbara Schenck, *Business Plans Kit For Dummies* (Hoboken, NJ: Wiley, 3rd ed., 2010), 11.

8. Erica Olsen, *Strategic Planning Kit For Dummies* (Hoboken, NJ: Wiley, 2nd ed., 2011), 15.

9. Tom Rath and Jim Harter, *Wellbeing: The Five Essential Elements* (New York: Gallup Press, 2010), 6.

10. Olsen, *Strategic Planning Kit For Dummies*, 36.

Chapter 1: WHY US:
The Current State of Parenting Affairs

1. Benjamin Spock, *The Commonsense Book of Baby and Child Care* (New York: Duell, Sloan & Pearce, 1946).

2. Jane E. Brody, "Final Advice from Dr. Spock: Eat Only All Your Vegetables," *New York Times*, June 20, 1998.

3. Eric Pace, "Benjamin Spock, World's Pediatrician, Dies at 94," *New York Times*, March 17, 1998.

4. Daniel J. Levitin, *The Organized Mind: Thinking Straight in the Age of Information Overload* (New York: Penguin, 2014).

5. J. Peder Zane, "In the Age of Information, Specializing to Survive," *New York Times*, March 19. 2015.

6. Laura A. Jana and Jennifer Shu, *Heading Home with Your Newborn: From Birth to Reality* (Elk Grove Village, IL: American Academy of Pediatrics, 3rd ed., 2015).

7. Simon Sinek, *Leaders Eat Last: Why Some Teams Pull Together and Others Don't* (New York: Penguin, 2014).

8. Nick Galifianakis, "Five Years," Nick and Zuzu, March 7, 2007.

9. Clayton Christensen and Derek van Bever, "The Capitalist's Dilemma," *Harvard Business Review*, June 2014.

10. Stephen Covey, *7 Habits of Highly Effective People* (New York: Simon & Schuster, 1990).

Chapter 2: WHY NOW:
The World Our Children Will Live In

1. Susan Sorenson, "Don't Pamper Employees—Engage Them," Gallup, July 2, 2013.

2. Kenneth R. Ginsburg, *Building Resilience in Children and Teens: Giving Kids Roots and Wings* (Elk Grove Village, IL: American Academy of Pediatrics, 2014).

3. A. G. Lafley and Roger L. Martin, *Playing to Win: How Strategy Really Works* (Boston: Harvard Business Publishing, 2013).

4. Bob Evans, "Global CIO: Google CEO Eric Schmidt's Top 10 Reasons Why Mobile Is #1," Government *InformationWeek*, April 14, 2010.

5. Tamar Lewin, "If Your Kids Are Awake, They're Probably Online," *New York Times*, January 20, 2010.

6. Rita McGrath, "Management's Three Eras: A Brief History," *Harvard Business Review*, July 30, 2014.

7. Claire Cain Miller, "Why What You Learned in Preschool Is Crucial at Work," *New York Times*, October 16, 2015.

8. Reid Hoffman and Ben Casnocha, *The Start-Up of You: Adapt to the Future, Invest in Yourself, and Transform Your Career* (New York: Crown Business, 2012), 5.

9. Rebecca J. Rosen, "Project Classroom: Transforming Our Schools for the Future," *The Atlantic*, August 29, 2011.

10. Thomas L. Friedman, "It's a 401(k) World," New York Times, April 30, 2013.

11. Simon Sinek, "How Great Leaders Inspire Action," filmed September 2009, TED video, 18:04.

12. Simon Sinek, *Start with Why: How Great Leaders Inspire Everyone to Take Action* (New York: Penguin, 2009).

13. "Mind the Gaps: The 2015 Deloitte Millennial Survey: Executive Summary," Deloitte.

14. Sorenson, "Don't Pamper Employees."

15. Ben Hecht, "Collaboration Is the New Competition," *Harvard Business Review,* January 10, 2013.

16. Miller, "Why What You Learned in Preschool Is Crucial at Work."

17. "The Principles," MIT Media Lab, accessed August 13, 2016.

18. Hoffman and Casnocha, *Start-Up of You,* 177.

Chapter 3: WHY EARLY: Baby Brain Science and the Foundational Importance of Starting Early

1. Congressional Record, V. 147, Pt. 3, March 8, 2001 to March 26, 2001, p. 4465.

2. Robert Fulghum, *All I Really Need to Know I Learned in Kindergarten: Uncommon Thoughts on Common Things* (New York: Random House, 1986).

3. Valerie Strauss, "Report Debunks 'Earlier Is Better' Academic Instruction for Young Children," *Washington Post,* April 12, 2015.

4. Lilian Katz, *Lively Minds: Distinctions between Academic versus Intellectual Goals for Young Children,* Defending the Early Years, 2015.

5. Rachel Saslow, "Teaching Babies to Read: Is It Possible? Several Companies Say Yes, But Study Says No," *Washington Post,* May 5, 2014.

6. "Elimination Communication," Wikipedia.

7. *Early Warning Confirmed: A Research Update on Third-Grade Reading,* Annie E. Casey Foundation, November 29, 2013.

8. "Important Milestones: Your Child at Two Years," Centers for Disease Control and Prevention, January 21, 2016.

9. P. L. Morgan, G. Farkas, M. M. Hillemeier, C. S. Hammer, and S. Maczuga, "24-Month-Old Children with Larger Oral Vocabularies Display Greater Academic and Behavioral Functioning at Kindergarten Entry," *Child Development* 86, no. 5 (September–October 2015): 1351–1370.

10. D. E. Jones, M. Greenberg, and M. Crowley, "Early Social-Emotional Functioning and Public Health: The Relationship between

Kindergarten Social Competence and Future Wellness," *American Journal of Public Health* 105, no. 11 (November 2015): 2283–2290.

11. W. Mischel and E. B. Ebbesen, "Attention in Delay of Gratification," *Journal of Personality and Social Psychology* 16, no. 2 (1970): 329–337.

12. Tom Wujec, "The Marshmallow Challenge," Tom Wujec (blog), www.marshmallowchallenge.com/Welcome.html.

13. Ray Villard, "The Milky Way Contains at Least 100 Billion Planets According to Survey," HubbleSite.org, January 11, 2012, archived from the original on July 23, 2014.

14. "Brain Architecture," Center on the Developing Child, Harvard University (website).

15. P. K. Kuhl, "Brain Mechanism in Early Language Acquisition," *Neuron* 67, no. 5 (September 2010): 713–727.

16. Joel Schwarz, "Brief Exposure to Mandarin Can Help American Infants Learn Chinese," University of Washington, February 17, 2003.

17. P. K. Kuhl, "Is Speech Learning 'Gated' by the Social Brain?" *Developmental Science* 10, no. 1 (2007): 110–120.

18. "Key Concepts: Serve and Return," Center on the Developing Child, Harvard University (website).

19. "Key Concepts: Executive Function and Self-Regulation," Center on the Developing Child, Harvard University (website).

20. Center on the Developing Child at Harvard University (2011). Building the Brain's "Air Traffic Control" System: How Early Experiences Shape the Development of Executive Function: Working Paper No. 11. Retrieved from www.developingchild.harvard.edu.

21. Center on the Developing Child at Harvard University, Building the Brain's "Air Traffic Control" System.

22. Adele Diamond, W. Steven Barnett, Jessica Thomas, and Sarah Munro, "Preschool Program Improves Cognitive Control," *Science* 318, no. 5855 (November 30, 2007): 1387–1388.

23. Center on the Developing Child at Harvard University, Building the Brain's "Air Traffic Control" System.

24. Center on the Developing Child at Harvard University, Building the Brain's "Air Traffic Control" System.

25. "Developmental Milestones," Centers for Disease Control and Prevention, accessed May 10, 2016.

26. Patricia Kuhl, "The Linguistic Genius of Babies," filmed October 2010, TED video, 10:17.

27. Pat Levitt, "Making the Case for Investing in Early Childhood" (keynote presentation, Child Trend's Building Our Future: Strategies

for Investing in Early Childhood convening supported by Robert Wood Johnson and George Kaiser Family Foundations, Tulsa, OK, May 2, 2016).

28. S. L. Calvert, B. L. Strong, E. L. Jacobs, and E. E. Conger, "Interaction and Participation for Young Hispanic and Caucasian Girls' and Boys' Learning of Media Content," *Media Psychology* 9 (2007): 431–445.

29. G. L. Troseth, M. M. Saylor, and A. H. Archer, "Young Children's Use of Video as a Source of Socially Relevant Information," *Child Development* 77, no. 3 (May–June 2006): 786–799.

30. Perks, "Emotional Intelligence: One of the Hottest Words in Corporate America," Perks Consulting, February 3, 2009.

31. Michael C. Frank, Edward Vul, and Scott P. Johnson, "Development of Infants' Attention to Faces during the First Year," *Cognition* 110, no. 2 (2009): 160–170.

32. Patricia K. Kuhl, "Early Language Acquisition: Cracking the Speech Code," *Nature Reviews Neuroscience* 5, no. 11 (2004): 831–843.

33. D. A. Anderson, J. Bryant, W. Wilder, A. Santomero, M. Williams, and A. M. Crawley, "Researching Blue's Clues: Viewing Behavior and Impact," *Media Psychology* 2 (2000): 179–194.

34. A. M. Crawley, D. R. Anderson, A. W. Wilder, M. Williams, and A. Santomero, "Effects of Repeated Exposures to a Single Episode of the Television Program Blue's Clues on the Viewing Behaviors and Comprehension of Preschool Children," *Journal of Educational Psychology* 91 (1999): 630–637.

35. R. Barr, R. Muentener, A. Garcia, M. Fujimoto, and V. Chavez, "The Effect of Repetition on Imitation from Television during Infancy," *Developmental Psychobiology* 49 (2007): 196–207.

36. T. Christina Zhao and Patricia K. Kuhl, "Musical Intervention Enhances Infants' Neural Processing of Temporal Structure in Music and Speech," *Proceedings of the National Academy of Sciences* 113, no. 19 (2016): 5212–5217.

37. Alison Gopnik, *The Philosophical Baby: What Children's Minds Tell Us about Truth, Love, and the Meaning of Life* (New York: Farrar, Straus and Giroux, 2009).

38. J. R. Saffran, R. N. Aslin, and E. L. Newport, "Statistical Learning by 8-Month-Old Infants," *Science* 274, no. 5294 (1996): 1926–1928.

39. Laura Schulz, "The Surprisingly Logical Minds of Babies," filmed March 2015, TED video, 20:18.

Part 2: QI Skills

1. "Yuán qì," Wikipedia.
2. "Qi," Wikipedia.
3. "What Is Quality Improvement?" Department of Community and Family Medicine, Duke University School of Medicine (website).

Chapter 4: QI Skill 1:
ME: Focusing Attention on Self-Management

1. "History," Keep Calm and Carry On, www.keepcalmandcarryon.com/history.

2. Francisco Sáez, "Peter Drucker, on Self-Management," Facile Things (blog), www.facilethings.com/blog/en/peter-drucker-self-management.

3. Daniel H. Pink, Drive: The Surprising Truth About What Motivates Us (New York: Riverhead Books, 2011).

4. Jim Collins, foreword to The Daily Drucker, by Peter Drucker (New York: HarperCollins, 2004).

5. Pink, Drive.

6. "Airport Yoga and Meditation Rooms: 5 U.S. Airport Spaces for On-the-Go Zen," Travel, Huffington Post, June 20, 2013.

7. Laszlo Bock, Work Rules!: Insights from Inside Google That Will Transform How You Live and Lead (New York: Hachette Book Group, 2015).

8. Kate Everson, "SAP's Sold on Self-Awareness," Chief Learning Officer, January 2, 2015.

9. "Stanford Marshmallow Experiment," Wikipedia.

10. Drake Bennett, "What Does the Marshmallow Test Actually Test?" Bloomberg, October 17, 2012.

11. B. J. Casey, L. H. Somerville, I. H. Gotlib, O. Ayduk, N. T. Franklin, M. K. Askren, J. Jonides, et al., "Behavioral and Neural Correlates of Delay of Gratification 40 Years Later," Proceedings of the National Academy of Sciences 108, no. 36 (July 2011): 14998–15003.

12. T. E. Moffitt, L. Arseneault, D. Belsky, N. Dickson, R. J. Hancox, H. Harrington, R. Houts, et al., "A Gradient of Childhood Self-Control Predicts Health, Wealth, and Public Safety," Proceedings of the National Academy of Sciences 108, no. 7 (February 15, 2011): 2693–2698.

13. Shael Polakow-Suransky and Nancy Nager, "The Building Blocks of a Good Pre-K," New York Times, October 21, 2014.

14. Angela Lee Duckworth, "Grit: The Power of Passion and Perseverance," filmed April 2013, TED video, 6:12.

15. L. Flook, S. B. Goldberg, L. Pinger, and R. J. Davidson, "Promoting Prosocial Behavior and Self-Regulatory Skills in Preschool Children through a Mindfulness-Based Kindness Curriculum," *Developmental Psychology* 5, no. 1 (January 2015): 44–51.

16. Ellen Galinsky, *Mind in the Making: The Seven Essential Life Skills Every Child Needs* (New York: HarperCollins, 2010), 32.

17. Galinsky, *Mind in the Making*, 26.

18. Rosemarie Truglio, PhD, phone conversation with the author, May 16, 2016.

19. Sam Stein, "The Scientist Who Taught Cookie Monster Self-Control Has a Warning for Congress," Politics, *Huffington Post*, September 18, 2015.

20. Deborah Linebarger, *Lessons from Cookie Monster: Educational Television, Preschoolers, and Executive Function*, Iowa Children's Media Lab, University of Iowa, 2014.

21. Linebarger, *Lessons from Cookie Monster*, 5.

22. Rosemarie Truglio PhD, phone conversation with author, May 16, 2016.

23. Sesame Street, "Me Want It (But Me Wait)," YouTube video, 3:10, August 5, 2013.

24. Chen Yu and Linda Smith, "The Social Origins of Sustained Attention in One-Year-Old Human Infants," *Current Biology* 26, no. 9 (May 9, 2016): 1235–1240.

25. D. J. Leong and E. Bodrova, "Assessing and Scaffolding Make-Believe Play," *Young Children* 67 no. 1 (2012): 28–34.

26. Elena Bodrova, Carrie Gemeroth, and Deborah J. Leong, "Play and Self-Regulation: Lessons from Vygotsky," *American Journal of Play* 6, no. 1 (2013): 111-123.

27. M. E. Schmidt, T. A. Pempek, H. L. Kirkorian, A. F. Lund, and D. R. Anderson, "The Effects of Background Television on the Toy Play Behavior of Very Young Children," *Child Development* 79 (2008): 1137–1151. doi: 10.1111/j.1467–8624.2008.01180.x.

28. Kelly April Tyrrell, "'Kindness Curriculum' Boosts School Success in Preschoolers," School of Education, University of Wisconsin–Madison, February 3, 2015.

29. Adele Diamond and Daphne S. Ling, "Conclusions about Interventions, Programs, and Approaches for Improving Executive Functions That Appear Justified and Those That, Despite Much Hype, Do Not," *Developmental Cognitive Neuroscience* 18 (2016): 34–48.

Chapter 5: QI Skill 2:
WE: Learning to Play Well with Others

1. "Pauline Phillips," Wikipedia.

2. Deborah Tannen, "Donahue Talked, Oprah Listened," New York Times, November 28, 2009.

3. Kiri Blakeley, "The Most Influential Women in Media," Forbes, July 14, 2009.

4. Marilyn Kennedy Melia, "Looking for 'People' People." Omaha World-Herald, December 6, 2015.

5. Suzy Kassem, Rise Up and Salute the Sun: The Writings of Suzy Kassem (Dubai, UAE: Awakened Press, 2011).

6. Reid Hoffman and Ben Casnocha, The Start-Up of You: Adapt to the Future, Invest in Yourself, and Transform Your Career (New York: Crown Business, 2012), 87–88.

7. "About Daniel Goleman," Daniel Goleman, http://www.daniel goleman.info/biography/.

8. Daniel Goleman, Emotional Intelligence: Why It Can Matter More Than IQ (New York: Bantam Dell, 1995).

9. Alison Gopnik, "'Empathic Civilization': Amazing Empathic Babies," The Blog (blog), Huffington Post, April 26, 2010.

10. Stephen Klasko, "What Doctors Aren't Learning in Medical School and Why It Matters," Forbes, July 27, 2015.

11. D. E. Jones, M. Greenberg, and M. Crowley, "Early Social-Emotional Functioning and Public Health: The Relationship between Kindergarten Social Competence and Future Wellness," American Journal of Public Health 105, no. 11 (November 2015): 2283–2290.

12. Rechele Brooks and Andrew N. Meltzoff, "The Development of Gaze Following and Its Relation to Language," Developmental Science 8, no. 6 (2005): 535–543.

13. Paul Tough, "Can the Right Kinds of Play Teach Self-Control?" New York Times, September 26, 2009.

Chapter 6: QI Skill 3:
WHY: Seeing the World as a Question Mark

1. Olivier Serrat, The Five Whys Technique (Manila, Philippines: Asian Development Bank, February 2009).

2. Serrat, Five Whys Technique.

3. Jeff Dyer, Hal Gregersen, and Clayton Christensen, The Innovator's

DNA: Mastering the Five Skills of Disruptive Innovators (Boston: Harvard Business Review Press, 2011), 77.

4. Peter Diamandis and Steven Kotler, *Abundance: The Future Is Better Than You Think* (New York: Simon & Schuster, 2012), 34.

5. David Sturt and Todd Nordstrom, "Are You Asking the Right Question?" *Forbes,* October 18, 2013.

6. Warren Berger, "Why Curious People Are Destined for the C-Suite," *Harvard Business Review,* September 11, 2015.

7. Berger, "Why Curious People Are Destined for the C-Suite."

8. Jeffrey H. Dyer, Hal Gregersen, and Clayton M. Christensen, "The Innovator's DNA," *Harvard Business Review,* December 2009.

9. Jeff Dyer, Hal Gregersen, and Clayton Christensen, *The Innovator's DNA: Mastering the Five Skills of Disruptive Innovators,* 71.

10. Jeffrey H. Dyer, Hal Gregersen, and Clayton M. Christensen, "The Innovator's DNA," *Harvard Business Review.*

11. Scott O. Lilienfeld and Hal Arkowitz, "Why 'Just Say No' Doesn't Work," *Scientific American,* January 1, 2014.

12. Jessica Lahey, "Educating an Original Thinker," *The Atlantic,* February 12, 2016.

13. Adam M. Grant, *Originals: How Non-Conformists Move the World* (New York: Penguin, 2016).

14. Jeff Dyer, Hal Gregersen, and Clayton Christensen, *The Innovator's DNA: Mastering the Five Skills of Disruptive Innovators,* 23.

15. Jeff Dyer, Hal Gregersen, and Clayton Christensen, *The Innovator's DNA: Mastering the Five Skills of Disruptive Innovators,* 74.

Chapter 7: QI Skill 4: WILL:
Self-Motivation: Applying the Power of WILL

1. "Harry Harlow 1905–1981," PBS, http://www.pbs.org/wgbh/aso/databank/entries/bhharl.html.

2. "Notable Research Completed at the Harlow Center: Dr. Harry Harlow," Harlow Center for Biological Psychology, University of Wisconsin–Madison (website).

3. "A History of Primate Experimentation at the University of Wisconsin, Madison–The early years: Harlow and 50 years of cruelty," Madison's Hidden Monkeys (website).

4. "Notable Research Completed at the Harlow Center: History," Harlow Center of Biological Psychology, University of Wisconsin-Madison (website).

5. Daniel H. Pink, Drive: The Surprising Truth About What Motivates Us (New York: Riverhead Books, 2011).

6. Pink, Drive.

7. Pink, Drive.

8. Pink, Drive.

9. Watty Piper, The Little Engine That Could (New York: Philomel Books, 2005)

10. Dave Coverly, "Speed Bump," cartoon, image no. 116565, September 25, 2014.

11. M. T. Greenberg, R. P. Weissberg, M. U. O'Brien, J. E. Zins, L. Fredericks, H. Resnik, and M. J. Elias, "Enhancing School-Based Prevention and Youth Development through Coordinated Social, Emotional, and Academic Learning," American Psychologist 58, no. 6/7 (2003): 466–474.

12. James Heckman, James Heckman Changes the Equation for American Prosperity (Chicago: Heckman Equation, 2013), 4.

13. Ellen Galinsky, Mind in the Making: The Seven Essential Life Skills Every Child Needs (New York: HarperCollins, 2010), 11.

14. Margaret Wise Brown, Goodnight Moon (New York: HarperFestival, 2007), 5.

Chapter 8: QI Skill 5: WIGGLE: Putting Wiggles to Work

1. Nilofer Merchant, "Got a Meeting? Take a Walk," filmed February 2013, TED video, 3:28.

2. Nilofer Merchant, "Sitting Is the Smoking of Our Generation," Harvard Business Review, January 14, 2013.

3. Henry David Thoreau, Thoreau: A Book of Quotations (Mineola, NY: Dover Publications, 2001).

4. M. Oppezzo and D. L. Schwartz, "Give Your Ideas Some Legs: The Positive Effect of Walking on Creative Thinking," Journal of Experimental Psychology: Learning, Memory and Cognition 40, no. 4 (2014): 1142–1152.

5. L. Bolz, S. Heigele, and J. Bischofberger, "Running Improves Pattern Separation during Novel Object Recognition," Brain Plasticity 1, no. 1 (2015): 129–141.

6. E. M. Hunter and C. Wu, "Give Me a Better Break: Choosing Workday Break Activities to Maximize Resource Recovery," Journal of Applied Psychology 10, no. 2 (2016): 302–311, doi:10.1037/apl0000045.

7. Charles H. Hillman, Kirk I. Erickson, and Arthur F. Kramer, "Be

Smart, Exercise Your Heart: Exercise Effects on Brain and Cognition," *Nature Reviews Neuroscience* 9, no. 1 (2008): 58–65.

8. Jeff Dyer, Hal Gregersen, and Clayton Christensen, *The Innovator's DNA: Mastering the Five Skills of Disruptive Innovators* (Boston: Harvard Business Review Press, 2011), 24.

9. Pooja S. Tandon, Brian E. Saelens, and Dimitri A. Christakis, "Active Play Opportunities at Child Care," *Pediatrics*, May 2015, doi:10.1542/peds.2014–2750.

10. M. Klaus and J. Kennel, "Commentary: Routines in Maternity Units: Are They Still Appropriate for 2002?" *Birth* 28, no. 4 (2001): 274–275.

11. Andrew N. Meltzoff and M. Keith Moore, "Imitation of Facial and Manual Gestures by Human Neonates," *Science* 198, no. 4312 (October 1977): 75–78.

12. Lea Winerman, "The Mind's Mirror," *Monitor on Psychology* 36, no. 9 (October 2005): 48.

13. Robert Kalan, *Jump, Frog, Jump!* (New York: Greenwillow Books, 1989).

14. Raffi, *Wheels on the Bus* (New York: Knopf Books for Young Readers, 1998).

Chapter 9: QI Skill 6: WOBBLE: Failing to Succeed: Raising Children Who Are Fit to Fail

1. "Weebles," Wikipedia.

2. Wendy Mogel, *The Blessing of a Skinned Knee: Using Jewish Teachings to Raise Self-Reliant Children* (New York: Penguin Group, 1988).

3. Kathy Chin Leong, "Google Reveals Its 9 Principles of Innovation," *Fast Company*, November 20, 2013.

4. Laszlo Bock, *Work Rules! That Will Transform How You Live and Lead* (New York: Hachette Book Group, 2015).

5. J. V. Matso, "Failure 101: Rewarding Failure in the Classroom to Stimulate Creative Behavior," *Journal of Creative Behavior* 25, no. 1 (March 1991): 82–85.

6. Tom Wujec, "Marshmallow Challenge," Design Projects Design Exercise, TED, February 4, 2015.

7. Tom Wujec, "Build a Tower, Build a Team," filmed February 2010, TED video, 6:51.

8. "'Bubble Boy' 40 Years Later: Look Back at Heartbreaking Case," CBSNews.

9. Carol Dweck, *Mindset: The New Psychology of Success* (New York: Ballantine Books, 2008).

Chapter 10: QI Skill 7: WHAT IF: Imagining a World of Possibilities

1. Kenneth Robinson, "Do Schools Kill Creativity?" filmed February 2006, TED video, 19:24.

2. Virginia Heffernan, "Education Needs a Digital-Age Upgrade," Opionionator (blog), *New York Times*, August 7, 2011.

3. Steve Denning, "What the Emerging Creative Economy Means for Jobs" (presentation, Innovation 4 Jobs [i4j] Summit, Stanford Research Institute [SRI], Palo Alto, CA, January 28, 2016).

4. Richard Florida, *The Rise of the Creative Class: And How It's Transforming Work, Leisure, Community, and Everyday Life* (New York: Basic Books, 2002).

5. Heffernan, "Education Needs a Digital-Age Upgrade."

6. Robinson, "Do Schools Kill Creativity?"

7. John Muir, "The National Parks and Forest Reservations," *Sierra Club Bulletin* 1, no. 7 (January 1896): 271–284.

8. Jean Piaget, speaking at a conference in Kyoto, Japan, 1971.

9. Creative Oklahoma, www.stateofcreativity.com/.

10. Kenneth Robinson, "All Our Futures: Creativity, Culture and Education" (presentation, 2015 World Creativity Forum, Thelma Gaylord Performing Arts Theater, Oklahoma City, OK, March 31, 2015).

11. Reid Hoffman and Ben Casnocha, *The Start-Up of You: Adapt to the Future, Invest in Yourself, and Transform Your Career* (New York: Crown Business, 2012), 3.

12. "IBM 2010 Global CEO Study: Creativity Selected as Most Crucial Factor for Future Success," news release, IBM, May 18, 2010.

13. Warren Berger, "Why Curious People Are Destined for the C-Suite," *Harvard Business Review*, September 11, 2015.

14. Creative Oklahoma, e-mail promotion for the annual Disney Institute and Rose State Partnership for Business Professionals and 1-Day Business Training from Disney Institute on the September 17, 2015.

15. "The World's 50 Greatest Leaders (2014)," *Fortune*, March 20, 2014.

16. Peter Diamandis, "Raising Kids during Exponential Times," Peter Diamandis (blog), 2015.

17. Bart Conner, "Ideas That Matter—an Oklahoma Experiment" (presentation, 2015 World Creativity Forum, Thelma Gaylord Performing Arts Theater, Oklahoma City, OK, March 31, 2015).

18. John S. Hutton, Tzipi Horowitz-Kraus, Alan L. Mendelsohn, Tom DeWitt, Scott K. Holland, the C-MIND Authorship Consortium, "Home Reading Environment and Brain Activation in Preschool Children Listening to Stories," *Pediatrics* 126, no. 3 (September 2015): 466–478.

19. Michele Root-Bernstein, "Imaginary Worldplay as an Indicator of Creative Giftedness," in *International Handbook on Giftedness*, ed. Larisa V. Shavinina (Dordrecht, the Netherlands: Springer Netherlands, 2009), 599–616.

20. Peter H. Reynolds, *Creatrilogy Box Set (Dot, Ish, Sky Color)* (Somerville, MA: Candlewick Press, 2012).

21. Jeanne E. Arnold, Anthony P. Graesch, Enzo Ragazzini, and Elinor Ochs, *Life at Home in the Twenty-First Century: 32 Families Open Their Doors* (Los Angeles: Cotsen Institute of Archaeology Press, 2012).

22. A. V. Sosa, "Association of the Type of Toy Used during Play with the Quantity and Quality of Parent-Infant Communication," *JAMA Pediatrics*, published online December 23, 2015, doi:10.1001/jamapediatrics.2015.3753.

23. Adele Diamond, quoted in Ellen Galinsky, *Mind in the Making: The Seven Essential Life Skills Every Child Needs* (New York: HarperCollins, 2010), 9.

24. Krista Tippett, "Transcript for Rex Jung: Creativity and the Everyday Brain," *On Being* (radio program), August 20, 2015.

Chapter 11: QI for All

1. UMass Boston, "Still Face Experiment: Dr. Edward Tronick," YouTube video, 2:48, filmed 2007, posted November 30, 2009.

2. Ryan White, "Language Gap between Rich and Poor Evident in Toddlers," USC Annenberg Center for Health Journalism, October 9, 2013.

3. Laura J. Colker, "The Word Gap: The Early Years Make the Difference," *Teaching Young Children* 7, no. 3 (2014): 26–28.

4. Center on the Developing Child at Harvard University (2011). Building the Brain's "Air Traffic Control" System: How Early Experiences Shape the Development of Executive Function: Working Paper No. 11. Retrieved from www.developingchild.harvard.edu.

5. James Heckman, "Going Forward Wisely" (presentation, White House Summit on Early Education, Washington, DC, December 15, 2014).

6. Shane J. Lopez, *Making Hope Happen: Create the Future You Want for Yourself and Others* (New York: Simon & Schuster, 2013).

7. Too Small to Fail, www.clintonfoundation.org/our-work/too-small-fail.

8. Vroom, www.joinvroom.org.

9. Zero to Three: National Center for Infants, Toddlers, and Families, www.zerotothree.org.

10. Thirty Million Words, www.thirtymillionwords.org.

11. ReadyNation, http://www.readynation.org.

12. The Heckman Equation, http://heckmanequation.org.

13. "Human Capital Research Collaborative National Invitational Conference Agenda," Human Capital Research Collaborative, https://humancapitalrc.org/news-and-events/2015-conference/conference2015-agenda.

14. Lopez, *Making Hope Happen*, 18.

15. Rose Pastore, "Read Mark Zuckerberg's Letter to His Newborn Daughter," *Fast Company*, December 1, 2015.

Acknowledgments

BEFORE ACKNOWLEDGING THE COLLEAGUES, FRIENDS, and family who contributed to collectively making this book a reality, let me first acknowledge something I admittedly paid very little attention to until I became an author: that taking the time to actually sit down, identify, and recognize in writing all of the caring, responsive people in one's life is no easy task. As soon as I attempted to do so, my list of names quickly became too long to fit on the number of pages typically allotted to an Acknowledgments section. While the following is thus abbreviated out of necessity, my sincere thanks go out to each and every one of you who has reinforced my belief in the importance of having caring, supportive people in one's life and my even stronger belief that all children deserve no less.

To both Reid Hoffman and Dr. Benjamin Spock, whose core beliefs and well-timed support at pivotal times in my professional life served to powerfully reinforce that I was on to something big.

For my mom, your lifetime of unwavering support and unconditional love gave me the strong foundation that got me (and this book) to where we are today. The example you set with a lifetime commitment to making the world a better place was icing on the cake!

To Jo Kirchner, first my CEO and now my colleague and friend, nothing is better than finding someone who shares the same drive, determination, and big-picture worldview.

Pediatricians Ari Brown, Michael Rich, Jennifer Shu, David Hill, Tanya Remer Altman, Alanna Levine, Sandy Hassink, and Harvey Karp—thanks for your input, support, comments, and, most of all, your shared commitment to improving the lives of all children.

For colleagues/friends Julia Cook, Victor Chan, Rosemary Wells, Tara Oakman, Bill Donovan, Rob Dugger, and Meg Small, I hope you know how fortunate I consider myself to have had our paths serendipitously cross and to get to collaborate with each of you.

Carol Russell, I can't thank you enough for being such a supportive cheerleader, confidante, and committed friend.

To Jennifer Pessini, the dedicated director of my child care center and good friend. Together we have had the pleasure of sharing ideas, challenges, and accomplishments.

A big thanks to TEDx Organizer Brian Smith and Niki Ernst for encouraging me to take to the TED stage and share the ideas that would eventually take further shape in this book.

Of course thanks also to my identical twin sister, Ellen Levy, for connecting me not only to Reid Hoffman, but also for her insights regarding many others in the worlds of business and innovation. My brother Philip Levy, friend Julie Biddlecombe, and many others definitely fall into the category of engaged and active listeners who motivated me to keep writing. And dad— thanks for not only listening, but for also making it a point to send my way the constant stream of potentially relevant interviews, books, and articles.

With respect to the daunting task of taking an idea and transforming it into the reality of a book, it was definitely a team effort—from the early support from my agent, Joelle Delbourgo, to my editor Dan Ambrosio and the entire team at Da Capo Lifelong Books. And to Bruce and Paige—your input along the way helped me more clearly lay out my thoughts and ideas.

For each of my many reviewers, I highly value the time you invested and the thoughts you shared to help make this ready for prime time.

And finally, none of this would have been possible without the love and support of my husband and children. Bethany, Alex, and Ryan—you are my motivation and my proudest achievement. The fact that Bethany actually sat by my side, read, and even helped edit my manuscript was one of the best parts of the whole process. For my husband, Ajoy—I said it before (see Dedication, in case you skipped that part) and I'll say it again: you deserve special recognition for more than twenty years of active listening and for being such a supportive husband and best friend—something that earns you my love and thanks, but also quite possibly the distinction of being the most knowledgeable orthopedic surgeon out there on the subject of early brain and child development—you're welcome!

Index

About the Author

DR. LAURA A. JANA IS a renowned pediatrician, health communicator, and award-winning parenting and children's book author. She holds faculty appointments at the University of Nebraska Medical Center's College of Public Health, where she serves as Director of Innovation, and at Penn State University's Edna Bennett Pierce Prevention Research Center. Recognized nationally for her more than two decades worth of promoting children's health and wellbeing and offering credible practical parenting advice to new and expectant parents, Dr. Jana serves as a trusted consultant for parents, national news media, academic and government organizations, non-profits, and major corporations.

Coming from a strong background in the biological sciences, Dr. Jana earned her Bachelor of Science degree in Cellular Molecular Biology at the University of Michigan, her MD from Case Western Reserve University, and completed her pediatric training at the University of California–San Francisco and at Rainbow Babies and Children's Hospital in Cleveland. She subsequently put her clinical training to good use in pediatric practices in Ohio, Virginia, and Nebraska. Having first served as a consultant to Dr. Benjamin Spock, Dr. Jana also went on to co-found The Dr. Spock Company—one of the first major online health sites—in the late 1990s, and subsequently her own company, Practical Parenting Consulting.

Professionally straddling the intersection between practical parenting and academia, and between health and education,

Dr. Jana has long been broadly focused on issues extending far beyond the four walls of a pediatric office, from education, community engagement, health technology and twenty-first century skill/workforce development to maternal child health, parenting, early brain and child development, injury prevention, immunization, and health and nutrition promotion/obesity prevention.

Firmly committed to helping all parents meet the earliest and most pressing needs of their children—especially those in poverty locally, nationally, and globally—Dr. Jana has also become actively involved in children's advocacy and driving the professionalization of and investment in early education and care in the U.S. through her work as a strategic consultant for the Robert Wood Johnson Foundation, as a member of Ready-Nation, and with Primrose Schools—first as the successful nine-year owner of Nebraska's first 200-student, AdvancEd-accredited educational child care center and subsequently as a national strategic consultant. She is an active member of the TED community, a longstanding Reach Out and Read advocate, and serves as an Early Childhood Champion and media spokesperson for the American Academy of Pediatrics.

And finally, in the spirit of practicing what she preaches, Dr. Jana considers her most important role to be that of proud mom and Chief Engagement Officer. She lives in Omaha, Nebraska, with her orthopedic surgeon husband and their three teenage children, and particularly enjoys photography, traveling to new places, sharing new ideas, and meeting interesting people.

To learn more about or connect with Dr. Jana, be sure to check out her website at www.drlaurajana.com, follow her on Twitter at @KidDocJana, and watch her 2014 TEDxOmaha talk entitled *Five Connections That Will Change Children's Lives.*